A Cultural History of the Native Peoples of Southern New England

Voices from

Past and Present

Moondancer  Strong Woman

Aquidneck Indian Council
Newport, Rhode Island, USA

Bäuu Press
Boulder, Colorado

Copyright © 1999, 2006 by Moondancer and Strong Woman, Aquidneck Indian Council, 12 Curry Avenue, Newport, RI 02840-1412, USA.

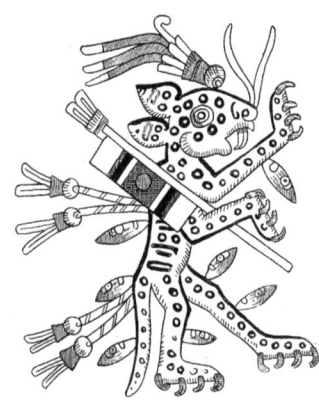

Bäuu Press

All rights reserved under International and Pan-American Copyright Conventions. No part of this book may be reproduced in any form or by any means without permission in writing from the publishers:
Bäuu Press, PO Box 4445, Boulder, CO. 80306.

Library of Congress Cataloging-in-Publication Data

A Cultural History of the Native Peoples of Southern New England: Voices from Past and Present
    / by   Francis Joseph O'Brien, Jr. (Moondancer)
            Julianne Jennings (Strong Woman)
        p. cm.

    Includes bibliographical references and index.
    ISBN 0-9721349-3-X   ISBN13 978-0-9721349-3-4
    1. Culture of Southern New England Indians. 2. Language of Southern New England Indians. 3. Contributions of Southern New England Indians. 4. New England Indian place names. I. The Massachusett Language Revival Project
    Library of Congress Catalog Card Number: 99-60829

Printed in the United States

10 9 8 7 6 5 4 3 2 1

A Cultural History of the Native Peoples of Southern New England
Voices from Past and Present

by

Moondancer  Strong Woman

Lord, who shall abide in thy tabernacle? Who shall dwell in thy holy hill?

He that walketh uprightly, and worketh righteousness, and speaketh the truth in his heart.
He that backbiteth not with his tongue, nor doeth evil to his neighbour, nor taketh up a reproach against his neighbour.
In whose eyes a vile person is contemned; but he honoureth them that fear the LORD. He that sweareth to his own hurt, and changeth not.
He that putteth not out his money to usury, nor taketh reward against the innocent. He that doeth these things shall never be moved.

Psalms, Chapter 15, *The Holy Bible*

Wunnohteaonk

MAY PEACE BE IN YOUR HEARTS

Credits and Acknowledgments

Peter Lenz generously allowed quotes throughout Chapter III from: *Volume I, Voyages to Norembega ca. 997-1621* (1994); *Skicinuwok Wanbanaghi or People of the Aurora*, 1621-1625, Vol. 2, Part 1 (1995); *Skicinuwok Wanbanaghi or People of the Aurora*, 1621-1625, Vol. 2, Part 2 (1995); *Skicinuwok Wanbanaghi: People of the Aurora*, 1621-1625, [Vol. 2,] Part 3. (1995). Norway, ME: Maine Performing Arts and Humanities, Inc.

Mary Benjamin generously gave permission to transcribe and quote selections throughout Chapter III from: *Princess Redwing, What Cheer Netop. History, Culture & Legends of the American Indians of the Northeast* (1986). (audio-cassette). South Casco, ME.

Cotton, Josiah (1830). "Vocabulary of the Massachusetts (Natick) Indian Language." Cambridge, MA: *Massachusetts Historical Society Collection, Serial 3, Vol. II*. [Courtesy Karl V. Teeter, Professor Emeritus of Linguistics, and Widener Library, Harvard University].

Eliot, John (1666). *The Indian Grammar Begun; or, an Essay to Bring The Indian Language into Rules for the Help of Such as Desire to Learn the Same for the Furtherance of the Gospel Among Them*. Cambridge, MA: Marmaduke Johnson [Courtesy of the John Carter Brown Library at Brown University].

Eliot, John & Thomas Mayhew (1834). "Tears of repentence: or, A further Narrative of the Progress of the Gospel Amongst the Indians in New-England". *Collections of the Massachusetts Historical Society*, 3rd. Ser. Vol. 4, pp. 197-287. [Courtesy of the John Carter Brown Library at Brown University].

R. F. Haffenreffer, Jr. "Indian History of Mount Hope and Vicinity". *Proceedings of Fall River Historical Society*, 1927 [Couretsy of Haffenreffer Museum of Anthropology, Brown University].

Figure 1. TRIBAL TERRITORIES ABOUT 1630. From *Handbook of North American Indians, Vol. 15 (Northeast)*, 1978, Washington, DC: Smithsonian Institution (p. 160). [Courtesy of Smithsonian Institution].

Figure 2. SOUTHERN NEW ENGLAND INDIAN SETTLEMENTS AND RESERVATIONS. From *Handbook of North American Indians, Vol. 15 (Northeast)*, 1978, Washington, DC: Smithsonian Institution (p. 178). [Courtesy of Smithsonian Institution].

Figure 3. MAP OF INDIAN LOCALITIES ABOUT NARRAGANSETT AND MOUNT HOPE BAYS. From *Sowans*, 1908, New Haven, CT: Associated Publishers of American Records. [Courtesy of Rhode Island Historical Society Library].

We acknowledge the following persons and institutions for assistance:

* Great Bear, Research Associate, Aquidneck Indian Council.
* Members and Directors, Aquidneck Indian Council.
* Rhode Island State Council on the Arts & Expansion Arts.
* Darrell Waldron, Executive Director, Rhode Island Indian Council.
* Numerous Newspaper Reporters in RI and MA..
* Professor Joel Cohen, History Department, University of Rhode Island.

CONTENTS

INTRODUCTION	1
Christianity and Early English Colonists	9
SOUTHERN NEW ENGLAND'S INDIAN CULTURE	13
Cultural History	14
Sources and Approach	17
CULTURAL OBSERVATIONS ARRANGED BY TOPIC	23
Their Appearance	25
Greeting and Language	31
Eating and Entertainment	37
Sleeping and Lodging	41
Numbers	45
Family and Relations	49
Domestic	53
The Body and Senses	59
Discourse and News and Oral History	61
Time	65
Seasons	67
Travel	69
The Heavens and Heavenly Bodies	73
Weather	75
The Winds	77
Birds	79
The Earth and Planting Crops	83
Helping the English	89

First Thanksgiving Day	91
Animals	93
The Sea	97
Fishing	99
Clothing	101
Religion	105
Government and Justice	117
Marriage	123
Wampum	127
Trade	129
Hunting	131
Games	135
War	137
Sickness	141
Death and Burial	143

APPENDICES

APPENDIX I. CONTRIBUTIONS OF THE NEW ENGLAND INDIANS TO AMERICA   147

APPENDIX II. TRANSLATION OF SOME INDIAN PLACE NAMES IN SOUTHERN NEW ENGLAND   153
Historic Southern New England Nations, Tribes, Villages   160
Reservations and Settlements and Other Places: Massachusetts   164
Reservations and Settlements and Other Places: Cape Cod   167
Reservations and Settlements and Other Places: The Islands   169
Other Names: Rhode Island   170
Other Names: Connecticut   173

APPENDIX III. SELECTED QUOTES FROM WRITINGS OF EARLY AMERICAN COLONISTS AND MODERN INDIAN ELDERS ON NATIVE WOMEN OF WAMANOAG, NARRAGANSETT AND MASSACHUSETT PEOPLES   175

APPENDIX IV. SELECTION OF SOME EUROPEANS WHO WROTE ABOUT NEW ENGLAND INDIANS IN THE 1500S, 1600S, AND 1700S   183

APPENDIX V. BRINGING BACK OUR LOST LANGUAGE   187

APPENDIX VI. PRONUNCIATION GUIDE	193
APPENDIX VII. WHITE HOUSE PROCLAMATION	205
REFERENCES AND SOURCES	207

LIST OF FIGURES

FIGURE 1. TRIBAL TERRITORIES ABOUT 1630	4
FIGURE 2. SOUTHERN NEW ENGLAND INDIAN SETTLEMENTS AND RESERVATIONS	5
FIGURE 3. MAP OF INDIAN LOCALITIES ABOUT NARRAGANSETT AND MOUNT HOPE BAYS	6
FIGURE 4. SOURCES OF INFORMATION FOR THE MASSACHUSETT LANGUAGE REVIVAL PROGRAM	192

LIST OF TABLES

TABLE 1. 17TH CENTURY POPULATION ESTIMATES	7

FOREWORD

As the second millennium begins, a tremendous revival of belonging is taking place among many American Indians in southeastern New England after so many years of struggle. Here in southeastern New England many people of Native American ancestry are sorting out the pieces of their humanness. Our Indian culture and language are coming back.

The proud and fiercely independent native peoples of southern New England once walked tall and proud on this land. Within a span of 60 years, only 400 (3%) of Wampanoag people, for example, survived the deadly foreign epidemics and King Philip's War (1675-1676). The survivors were confined to reservations, plantations, and settlements within a Colonial culture and government throughout Rhode Island, Massachusetts, and Connecticut. Then, little by little, the structure of traditional Indian culture was annihilated. The forces of disease, blood mixing, enactment of law, racist attitude, and isolation have disintegrated the looks, language, and lore of the regional Indians. The essence of traditional Indian Spirituality—the Indian language—fell silent about 100-200 years ago on the mainland of Wampanoia.

For so long many people of Indian ancestry have been burdened with shame. We have had to deny to others and ourselves that we come from an ancient civilization that survived here on Turtle Island for over 10,000 years.

Very few books on our history and culture have been written by Indians themselves. Most standard academic books read like a clinical autopsy of a dead culture with big words few can understand.

The Aquidneck Indian Council was founded by local Native Americans representing several Algonquian Wapanachki tribes. We were formed to produce programs and publications that tell our story and help bring back our ancient language. We operate on a (broken) shoestring budget, but our efforts are spiritual and we will continue to honor the Spirits of the First North American Peoples. This book is one publication from our Council. It is our Millennium memorial to our people.

This book you are about to read provides an understanding of the ways, customs, and language of the southern New England Indians—from voices of our modern Elders and other Indians, and from historic records of the 1500s and 1600s. Everything you ever heard about the beauty, the power, and richness of our culture has been included. We hope you enjoy this book.

May the Indian People live! Let it be that way.
With love in our hearts, we are humbly,

Moondancer   Strong Woman

Newport, Rhode Island
February, 1999
November, 2005

Aho!

They want to dry the tears that drowned the sun.
They want laughter to return to their hearts.
They want to go home—to Mother and Grandmother.
They want to hear their ancestral voices 'round the fire.

INTRODUCTION

This is the story of the native peoples of southern New England. We start our story with the Wampanoag Indians—the first native peoples encountered by the Europeans and among the best documented tribes of southern New England. Their history and culture mirrors that of other regional people. The Wampanoag Indians are the First Americans of Rhode Island and Massachusetts. They are an ancient civilization and they have been here forever. They will remain as long.

In December, 1620 the ship *The Mayflower* came to our shores. When the English walked upon the beach of Cape Cod, they entered a village we called *Patuxet* (place of the little falls). No one lived there at the time. The people had perished from catastrophic diseases brought by previous European explorers.

There were 102 English men, women and children, all cold, tired and hungry who came ashore on our land. They were soon welcomed by our people. We befriended them. We helped these poor people in many ways. Without our knowledge, intelligence and skills and our kindness and our generosity, these strangers would surely have perished from the cold and lack of food.

The English strangers would call us by many names in their daily speech, their diaries, letters, journals and sermons. They called us by disrespectful names like *wildmen, pagans, savages, heathens, barbarians* and other such terms. To them these words meant they believed that we were racially inferior to them. Sometimes they would call us by a tribal name they invented—*Pawkunnawkutts* (Pokanokets). This word referred to the village-region that our great leader Massasoit and his family lived—*pauqu'unahkeet*, meaning "where the land is clear and open" (Moondancer & Strong Woman, 1996). Later appeared the word *Wampanoag*. The word *Wampanoag* means "People of the First Light" or "Easterners".

We called ourselves simply "the people," "the human beings," or "we who are all alike." In our language, we would say *nnínnuog*.

In days of old maybe up to 100,000 or more full-blooded, Algonquian-speaking native peoples lived in southern New England, from Cape Cod and beyond to the Hudson River. One of the oldest and most quoted European recorders of events in the 1600s (Daniel Gookin) tells us that:

> The principal nations of the Indians, that did, or do, inhabit within the confines of New-England, are five: 1. Pequots; 2. Narragansitts; 3. Pawkunnawkuts; 4. Massachusetts; and 5. Pawtuckets. (Gookin, 1674, p. 9)

Gookin apparently includes Mohegans among the Pequots, and the Nipmucks among the Massachusetts. See Figure 1 below for a map.

The reader will note that in those days the Wampanoag were called Pawkunnawkutts (Pokanoket in modern spelling) by the English. Spellings vary considerably from one document to another in the Colonial period. Within the same document, we can see a same name spelled 2 or 3 different ways as if the writer losses his memory the more he continues the writing [the English also consumed huge amounts of alcohol daily which could account for their mistakes]. This is generally the case for Colonial primary-source material as written by English-men of this day, who, by today's standards would be called uneducated, or illiterate, and many would be considered seriously alcohol-dependent (a ruinous disease passed on to our ancestors).

Now, Daniel Gookin, who was a high ranking government official in Massachusetts Bay Colony, also gives us these words about the Pawkunnawkutts (Wampanoag):

> The Pawkunnawkutts [Wampanoags] were a great people heretofore. They lived to the east and northeast of the Narragansitts; and their chief sagamore [The Massasoit] held

dominion over divers other petty sagamores; as the sagamores upon the island of Nantucket, and Nope, or Martha's Vineyard, of Nawsett, of Mannamoyk, of Sawkattukett, Nobsquasitt, Matakees, and several others, and some of the Nipmucks. Their country, for the most part, falls within the jurisdiction of New Plymouth colony. These people were a potent nation in former times; and could raise, as the most credible and ancient Indians affirm, about three thousand men. They held war with the Narragansitts; and often joined with the Massachusetts, as friends and confederates against the Narragansitts. This nation, a very great number of them, were swept away by an epidemical and unwonted sickness, An. [in the years] 1612 and 1613, about seven or eight years before the English arrived in these parts, to settle the colony of New Plymouth. Thereby divine providence made way for the quiet and peaceable settlement of the English in those nations. What this disease was, that so generally and mortally swept away, not only these, but other Indians, their neighbors, I cannot well learn. Doubtless it was some pestilential disease. I have discoursed with some old Indians, that were then youths; who say, that the bodies all over were exceedingly yellow, describing it by a yellow garment they showed me, both before they died, and afterward. (Gookin, 1674, p. 8)

This sample about the Wampanoag from Gookin shows why the Colonial records are so important for understanding the past, as well as the limitations of European knowledge about the southern New England Indians.

Maps will help in organizing the discussion[1]. The map on the following page (Figure 1) gives some indication of the ancient tribal territories in southern New England mentioned by Gookin. The broad white line shows tribal boundaries. For example, the region in the lower right-hand corner of the map labeled *Pokanoket* is the ancient homeland of the entire Wampanoag Nation. The Wampanoag Nation included all of Cape Cod, Martha's Vineyard, and Nantucket and other islands.

The regional Indian people comprised many tribes, bands and villages. For instance, some have said that there were over 300 villages with 30 to 50 major tribal groupings in the Wampanoag ter-

---

1. A translation of the Indian place names on these maps (and some not on them) is given in Appendix II. Most of these places no longer have Indian names since their homelands were stolen and renamed. The book by Huden (1962) is a good source for Indian place names in New England.

ritory shown in Figure 1. No one knows for certain because so many people died during European-introduced epidemics, and the barrier of language existing between the English and the local indigenous population made it difficult for the English to understood what they were told.

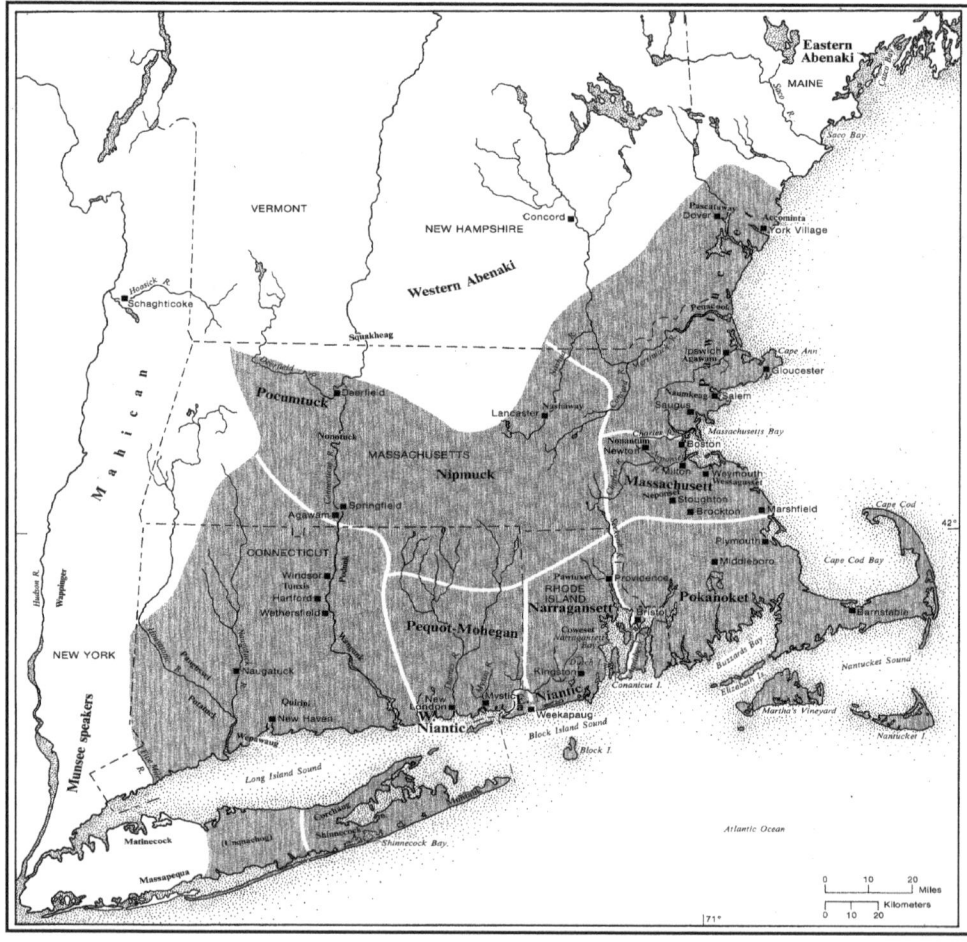

Figure 1. The broad white lines show tribal territories (ancestral homelands). A black square indicates a modern non Indian town. A large bold-type name refers to an Indian Nation (e.g., Massachusett), the smaller bold-type names indicate tribal subdivisions (e.g., Neponset). Present day State boundaries are indicated by dashed lines — - — -   and State names are capitalized (e.g., MASSACHUSETTS), and geographical features are italicized (e.g., *Atlantic Ocean*). Source: Bruce G. Trigger (Volume Editor). 1978. *Handbook of North American Indians, Vol. 15 (Northeast)*, Washington, DC: The Smithsonian Institution (Page 160). Used with permission.

Figure 2 (a very busy map) shows the general situation after the year 1674 with the names of many Indian settlements. We note that certain places where major groups of the Wampanoag had villages such as Mount Hope and the Seaconke locations (Watchemoquit, Wannamoisett, and others) are not listed. A more fine grained map is given next, Figure 3 (Bicknell, 1908), which focuses on the lands occupied by the Wampanoag at and near the Massasoit's villages in Sowams ("south country").

Figure 2. Black squares indicate a modern non Indian town, present day State boundaries are indicated by dashed lines — - — - . State names are capitalized (e.g., MASSACHUSETTS), and geographical features are italicized (e.g., *Atlantic Ocean*). Source: Bruce G. Trigger (Volume Editor). 1978. *Handbook of North American Indians, Vol. 15 (Northeast)*, Washington, DC: The Smithsonian Institution (Page 178). Used with permission.

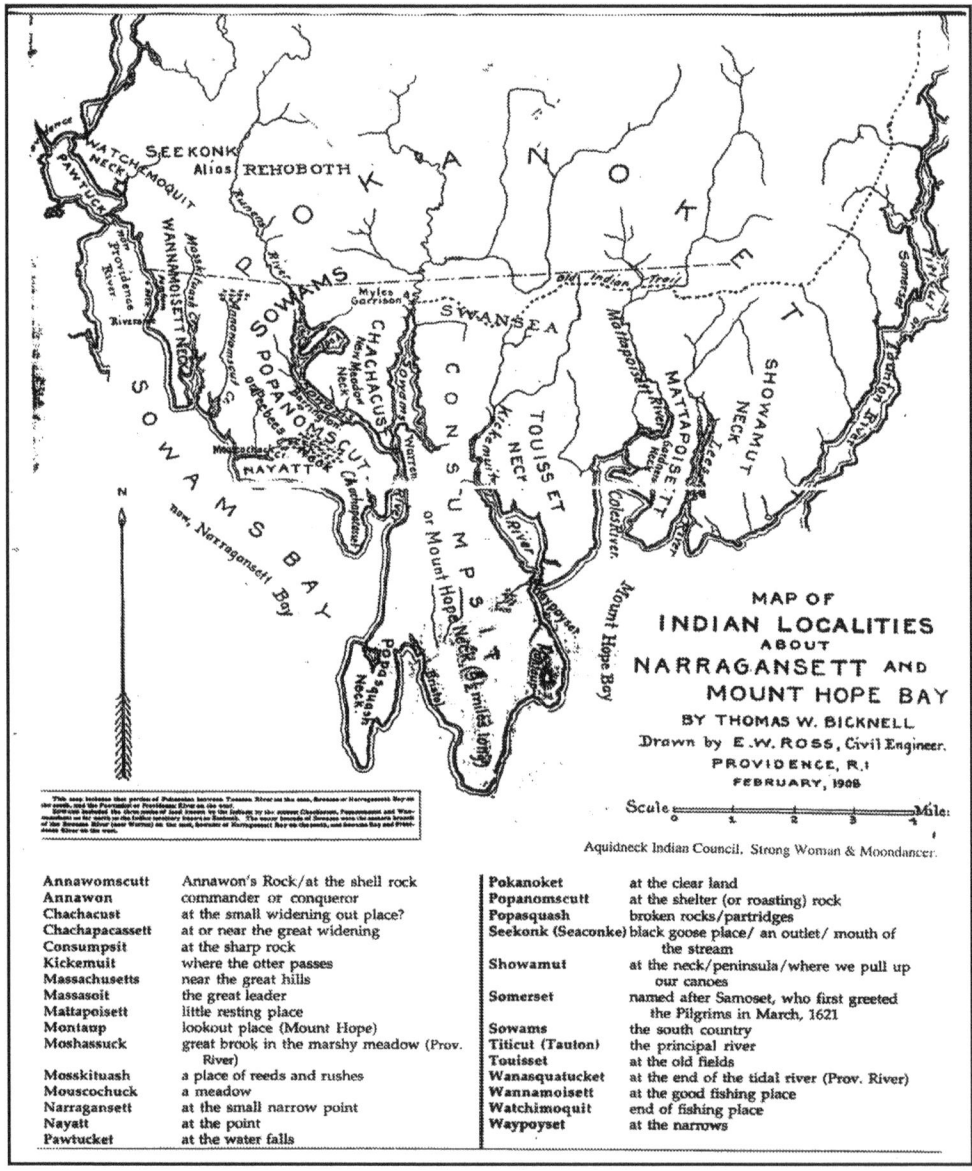

Figure 3. MAP OF INDIAN LOCALITIES ABOUT NARRAGANSETT AND MOUNT HOPE BAYS. Source: Bicknell, Thomas W. 1908. *Sowams*. New Haven, CT: Associated Publishers of American Records. [Courtesy of the Rhode Island Historical Society Library].

The number of full-blooded Indians living in each of these nations obviously is not known with any certainty. One set of population estimates is given in the following table. The idea behind these calculations is very simple. Gookin mentions that the Pokanoket had 3,000 warriors (by his guess and based on his meager knowledge of the Indian language). If we assume each biological family had 4 people (a mother, a father, 1 son, 1 daughter), then 4 people/family x 3000 warriors = 12, 000 people.

Table 1. 17th Century Population Estimates (Before Epidemics)

NATION	ESTIMATED POPULATION
Pokanoket/Wampanoag	12,000
Narragansett	20,000
Pequot/Mohegan	16,000
Massachusett	12,000
Pawtucket	12,000

Source: Gookin, 1674; quoted in Bragdon, p. 25.

The numbers in Table 1 are not the result of an accurate census of the ancient ancestors living here. They were not obtained by the scientific method of statistical enumeration, and we don't know how to grade the truthfulness or accuracy of many of the old documents written by English-men who, by and large, hated the people they were bent on stealing from.

The numbers are "ball park" estimates that historians have come to accept (such as Bragdon, 1996). Some scholars put the Pokanoket/Wampanoag number as high as 35,000, and the Massachusetts (including the Nipmucks) as high as 45,000, and the Narragansetts as high as 30,000 (Bonfati, 1993). No one knows for sure. If 3,000 is the correct number of warriors for the Wampanoag, then certainly 12,000-15,000 is a reasonable range. If we assume 5 people/family, then 3,000 x 5 = 15,000.

Several devastating epidemics between 1612-1619 brought by European explorers reduced the Indian populations along the coast by up to 90% of the original population. When the Pilgrims landed at Plymouth (Patuxet) in 1620, fewer than 2,000 mainland

Wampanoag had survived out of the original population of up to 12,000-15,000. The island people, especially the Wampanoag, were protected somewhat by their relative isolation and still had 3,000. At least 10 major mainland villages had been abandoned after the epidemics. After the English Puritan settlement of modern-day Massachusetts in 1630, epidemics continued to reduce the mainland Wampanoag until there were only 1,000 by 1675. Additional factors further reduced the Wampanoag even more, such as causalities in the King Philip's War, enslavement and shipment to other lands, and escape to other tribes. Historians point out that many Indians fled the area and found a new home among the St. Francis band of the Abenaki in Canada where they intermarried and remained.

It is believed that only 400 Wampanoag survived King Philip's War in 1676 and remained in this region. That is, in a span of less than 60 years, up to 98% of the proud and fiercely independent Wampanoag Indians were destroyed by the Europeans who came to this land in search of God and gold and glory. This survival rate is similar in other tribal groups of southern New England.

Now, some scholars have said the 1600s was perhaps the worst century in all of European history. For Indian people, this has turned out to be a true statement.

The Dream was ended
The Circle was broken
The People became enslaved
Mattanitoog (the Demons) had come
as prophesied by The Old Ones

In the 1600s, the average European probably lived to be about 30 years old, and today non Indians enjoy life into their 70s. In ancient times Indians lived to be about 60 years old due to their healthy, natural and happy lifestyle. Today, the typical person of Indian descent rarely reaches his, her 50th birthday. The American Indians are the poorest people in the land. The US Government promised to feed, house, cloth and care for the native peoples, in exchange for giving up their land and culture. These promises have turned out to be lies. What does this say about our national honor?

Great, great crimes against humanity have taken place on this land—crimes which are unnamed, uncounted and unweighed! Our prestige and honor depend on how we treat our aboriginal people—the original mothers and fathers of this country.

Our national honor is at stake. Throughout history, mighty civilizations—from ancient Egypt, Greece, Rome and others—have risen and they have fallen. One day the United States of America may find her equal on the battlefield or in the sky or sea. How will our now powerful enemies treat us? Our enemies may wonder out loud—where is your honor, America? They may deal with us partly based on this assessment of our history. Thus, in the eyes of the world, is the Government of the United States of America viewed as one of liars, thieves and murderers?

This is what President Clinton said in his National American Indian Heritage Month Proclamation:

> ... many people who live in Indian Country are caught in a cycle of poverty made worse by poor health care and a lack of educational and employment opportunity. *If we are to honor the United States Government's long-standing obligations to Indian tribes*, we must do all in our power to ensure that American Indians have access to the tools and opportunities they need to make the most of their lives. (President Clinton, Oct. 29, 1998; italics added)

CHRISTIANITY AND EARLY ENGLISH COLONISTS

The English were Protestant Christians. Their whole life was based on following the teachings in their religious book called The Holy Bible. Their great teacher was called Jesus Christ, the Son of God. God the Father made His son into a man (usually seen as White!) and sent him to live among the human race for 33 years, to bring the Good News of Christianity to all people on earth. He taught his followers—called Christians—to love all people no matter what their skin color was, where they lived, or how they looked or dressed. "Love thy neighbor as thyself"—that is the essence of the worldly teachings of Jesus Christ.

In the Christian Faith, a person who lives in accordance with the Teachings of Jesus Christ as revealed in the Bible is rewarded with eternal happiness in Heaven. Sinners are cast into the The Lake of Fire to suffer for all time. Non-Christians, by definition, do not go to Heaven (like Indians).

The Christians believed there was an answer for everything in this book. Their ministers would say what God meant when it was hard to understand the words in the Bible. The ministers were special agents of God. But the King of England was second-in-charge of the Universe, answering only to God. The English King decided what God said and meant. Apparently, the King believed God had given him and England all the land in the world which was not occupied by Christians. For example, they thought the Bible said that this land we call the USA really belonged to the Christians because only Christians were allowed to live here. The Bible does not teach these lies. Also, some thought it was required to convert others to Christianity—no matter what the cost.

Jesus Christ did not teach his followers to steal land from God's other children. He did not tell anyone it was his father's will to trick people into giving over their land when they were first made drunk, and then lied to about what making marks on paper meant. Or threatened with death if they did not do what the English wanted them to do in the name of Jesus Christ.

So, the English could take our land and some became really rich. Some of our most prominent and wealthy families in RI, MA, and CT today are descended from the first English. They became rich this way. Apparently the Christian teachings of the early English were not working for them when they came here. So, we believe that the English really came here for three reasons:

> 1. Religious freedom for themselves;
> 2. To escape the filth, crime, disease, poverty, overcrowding in England;
> 3. Become wealthy off the Indians based on wrong beliefs about the teachings of Jesus Christ.
> Their wealth has meant our poverty.

We also think that the English who came here did not live in accordance with the Teachings of Jesus Christ. They violated the Commandants of God. The Christian Faith teaches the following from *The Holy Bible*, the same teachings given to Indians:

<> Lay not up for yourselves treasures upon earth, where moth and rust doth corrupt, and where thieves break through and steal.
<> But lay up for yourselves treasures in heaven, where neither moth nor rust doth corrupt, and where thieves do not break through nor steal.
<> For where your treasure is, there will your heart be also.
<> The light of the body is the eye: if therefore thine eye be single, thy whole body shall be full of light.
<> But if thine eye be evil, thy whole body shall be full of darkness. If therefore the light that is in thee be darkness, how great is that darkness!
<> No man can serve two masters: for either he will hate the one, and love the other; or else he will hold to the one, and despise the other. Ye cannot serve God and mammon.
<u>Matthew, Chapter 6</u>

<> *Then said Jesus unto his disciples, Verily I say unto you, That a rich man shall hardly enter into the kingdom of heaven.*
<> *And again I say unto you, It is easier for a camel to go through the eye of a needle, than for a rich man to enter into the kingdom of God.*
<u>Matthew, Chapter 19</u>

These universal teachings are 2,000 years old. "Thou shalt not kill" does not mean it was OK to kill Indians because they were not White or did not follow the Christian Faith. "Thou shalt not steal" does not mean it was OK to steal an Indian's land. The English who did not live in accordance with these teachings insulted the Will of God. They have been dealt with in the religion of their faith. Have the Souls of most of the early English been confined to the Lake of Fire, chased around eternally by Red Men carrying spears?

ENGLISH	ALGONQUIAN
Thou shalt not kill	Nusheteokon
Thou shalt not steal	Kommootuhkon
Thou shalt not bear false witness against they neighbour	Pannoowae wauwaonuhkon ketatteamuk
Thou shalt not covet they neighbour's house, thou shalt not covet they neighbour's wife, nor his manservant, nor his maidservant, nor his ox, nor his ass, nor anything that is thy neighbor's	Ahchewontogkon
Exodus, Chapter 20	Josiah Cotton, 1830, p. 249

SOUTHERN NEW ENGLAND INDIAN CULTURE

People often ask—how much did local Indians in southern New England change over the years as a result of contact with European diseases, alcohol, Christianity, slavery, racism, discrimination, inter marrying, technological changes and the like—in short, all of the influences of acculturation and assimilation? To partially answer this question, we quote one of the most respected scholars on local Indians:

> Most scholars agree ... that Native American life changed dramatically as a result of contact, yet many modern ethnographers and historical treatments also stress the persistence of Native American identity and society. (Bragdon, 1996, p. 238)

When the King Philip's war ended in 1676, the People and their ways seemed destined for extinction. Little by little, the structure of traditional Indian culture was annihilated. The forces of disease, blood mixing, enactment of law, racist attitude, and isolation have disintegrated the looks, language and lore of the southern New England Indians. The essence of Indian spirituality—the ancient Indian language—fell silent about 100-200 years ago on the mainland (Huden, 1962).

However, one sees today marriages, burials, council meetings, powwows, social gatherings, sacred tobacco ceremonies, sweats, and the like, which, although modified and adapted over the years, nonetheless embrace *nukkône mayash* — the ways of the ancient ones[2]. The Wampanoag and other tribes in southern New England are reconstructing their language spoken in these woods, fields, lakes and mountains for over 10,000 years (Moondancer Strong Woman, 1996; Strong Woman Moondancer, 1998d). We are now able to say prayers and sing songs in the ancient language.

CULTURAL HISTORY

It is now time to turn to our main focus, a brief cultural history of the Indian people of this region through original sources, both European and Indian. Who were the full-blooded Indians who lived in many *otanash* (villages) almost 400 years ago in the areas shown in Figure 1? What were their customs, their ways? How did they govern themselves? How did they record their history? What was their manner of hunting, fishing, telling time, marrying, and many more things? We can obtain insight into these questions by listening to our Elders and other Indians and from reading writers who observed and lived among the full-blooded Algonquians in the 1500s & 1600s and recorded their cultural ways.

Very few records exist documenting the words of native peoples in historic times. Thus, for example, if one desires to know about the causes and events of the King Philip's War (1675-1676), all that is available are the words of the conquering Europeans whose words sometimes seem like the "look-how-big-a-fish-I-caught-today" stories not meant to be taken seriously. The native people do not speak from the past on these events. Thus, we have available only the writings of Europeans.

We do have the words of our modern Elders such as Princess Red Wing and others. Their wisdom has been passed down to them through oral tradition from the Elders. The traditional legends, stories and prayers are very important for understanding the customs and ways of the Wampanoag. Most books omit these crucial sources of knowledge.

---

2. Appendix I discusses the contributions and legacies of New England Indians to our country.

The Europeans of the 1500s and 1600s recorded a great deal about what they observed among the native peoples of New England. See Appendix IV for major European writers of this period. Some of these European men lived in the native villages and observed first hand many of the ways of Algonquian speaking people. Some—like Roger Williams and John Eliot—learned a significant amount of the complicated Algonquian languages, facilitating communication. The reader must realize that the Algonquian people of southern New England all spoke dialects of the same Algonquian language and shared similar social, political and religious practices. But it would be a mistake to assume that all the native peoples of southern New England were identical in all of their cultural beliefs and practices. We recommend the recent book by Kathleen J. Bragdon (1996) for those who want to learn more about these specific differences between different tribes or nations. Bragdon's book is scholarly in nature, but it is an objective, cultured work which portrays the native peoples in their own light and right. We were careful to select cultural practices and beliefs known or believed to be common among the different people of southeastern New England or which sheds some light on general characteristics of the local people. Some of these cultural practices have survived down through the centuries and are used today on an intertribal basis.

One very important reason for our unique approach is to put down on paper words and perceptions and thoughts so that readers can form their own judgment in light of modern experiences in American civilization. The American population has achieved a degree of education and culturedness for this to be a real challenge in understanding our own history. Is the United States of America a Nation of Honor in its dealings and treatment of the American Indian since the early 1600s? Do some worship and admire and name schools and parks, etc. after early Englishmen who are probably in Hell for their perfidious crimes against humanity? In this era of Cultural Diversity, when such questions are encouraged, is the time to tackle these questions.

Much modern material has been written on the culture of the Wampanoag and related Algonquian speaking people (e.g., Trigger, 1978; Bragdon, 1996). The approach taken in the present book is different. We present material exclusively from first hand sources, by our modern Elders, and by people who lived in the 1500s and 1600s, who lived among and knew of the culture of the Wampanoag and related Algonquian peoples of southeastern New England, and wrote of what they witnessed and understood (or misunderstood). By judicious selection of the primary sources it is possible to gain some insight into Indian culture. Descriptions of hunting practices from the 1500s and 1600s, for example, are more reliable and readily understood than descriptions of religion. It is easier to describe what one sees and easily understands (like hunting deer or color of hair) as opposed to explaining what one observes in healing ceremonies or religious practices which are totally novel (and scary?) to the observer.

The European's biases of the 1500s and 1600s (and beyond) must be taken into account when interpreting the observations in the next section. Even the best friends of the native peoples (like Roger Williams) uses words like "barbarians" and "savages" when referring to them! (*Records of the Colony of Rhode Island and Providence Plantations, in New England*, Vol. I, 1636-1663.) Another "friend" of the southern New England Indians was Daniel Gookin, "Superintendent of the Indians," a government magistrate of Massachusetts Colony (a sort of modern-day Bureau of Indian Affairs Head). His official government account of the traditional Wampanoag and other Indians in the region says in part:

> The customs and manners of these Indians were, and yet are, in many places brutish and barbarous in several respects, like unto other savage people of America [Indians] .... They are very revengeful, and will not be unmindful to take vengeance upon such as have injured them or their kindred .... They are much addicted to idleness, especially the men .... They are naturally much addicted to lying and speaking untruth; and unto stealing, especially from the English.... (Gookin, 1674, p. 9)

These characterizations are the "official" history recorded on this land and seem to be widely held views even among the most cultured Protestant Christian Europeans at the time. In some places these words from Gookin have become historical and anthropological facts to be memorized like Newton's Laws of Motion (these biases continue to exist in our society). Some other European writers, especially the ministers like Increase Mather, seemed to be consumed by utter fear & hatred, and to be in a state of hysteria and rage when discussing our people—akin to Nazi Propaganda Minister Dr. Josef Goebbels when he gave speeches about the Jews in the 1930s and 1940s. Such misconceptions, fears, prejudices and outright untruths, was one reason that motivated us to write the present book. We believe that the history of the Wampanoag people and other First Americans of lower New England should be presented in a wider context shorn of the prejudices, the terror and hysteria, the racist mentality and absolute religious hatred of the Colonial "visible saints" from "the city on the hill."

SOURCES AND APPROACH

In the following chapter we acquaint the reader with major aspects of the ways, customs and cultural characteristics of the Wampanoag Indians and related peoples from both of these sources: the old historic records of Europeans and our modern Elders and other Indians. A total of 33 areas were selected from which to summarize the cultural observations.

Our major sources of European writers who lived and wrote in the 1500s & 1600s are: Giovanni da Verrazzano, Roger Williams, Thomas Morton, William Wood, Daniel Gookin, William Bradford, and Edward Winslow[3]. More information on these writers' backgrounds may be found in Bragdon, 1996, pp. 7-14. The names of the works of our primary sources are listed in the References section. Other works shown there are important sources on other aspects of regional Indian history and culture. Appendix IV lists other important European writers and other sources to look into for additional information.

The modern sources are from our Elders who pass on history, culture and all the stories and legends and prayers & songs that have been kept in the Indian community over the centuries. Other material comes from other tribal people.

On the following pages we give quotes from the above-men-

---

3. It should be pointed out that many quotes from the works of Giovanni da Verrazzano, William Wood, Thomas Morton, William Bradford, Edward Winslow and in the work *Mourt's Relation*, come from the monumental efforts of Maine historian Peter Lenz, who for more than 20 years has gone all over the world recording these words and maps from the earliest times. The Aquidneck Indian Council is grateful to Mr. Lenz for allowing us to quote liberally from his works. See Appendix IV at the back of the book for a list of other Europeans to look into. Mr. Lenz's address is given there.

tioned sources which portray aspects of regional Indian culture. The observations are arranged by topic (Appearance, Greeting & Language, Eating and Entertainment, etc.). Each entry gives the source from which the 16th and 17th century material and the modern material was taken. For example, after one quote we write—(Wm. Wood, 1634; quoted in Lenz, 1995b, pp. 67-68). This means that the quote comes originally from the book written by William Wood in the year 1634, and was reprinted on pages 67-68 by Lenz in one of his books that he wrote in 1995.

In the case of Roger Williams, several editions of the original 1643 work—*A Key into the Language of America*—have been printed over the years. The quotes in our book from the 1643 Roger Williams classic may be found readily in any edition of the work, since we follow closely the chapter headings used by him. For example, our section on Hunting corresponds to R. Williams' chapter with the same basic heading (*Of their Hunting, &c.*).

As for the modern material, we have taken much wisdom from our great Elder, Princess Red Wing of the House of Seven Crescents. Selections from her 1986 audio-cassette tape were transcribed[4]. The traditional material was set down from memory from the oral tradition of Strong Woman.

An intimate part of regional culture is the ancient, sleeping language called Massachusett. Many of our citations contain the language. Our language has been lost, some say, for about 200 years on the mainland. The Aquidneck Indian Council's program—The Massachusett-Narragansett Language Revival Program—publishes pronunciation, vocabulary and grammar lessons. For additional information on language, we refer the reader to our recent book, *Understanding Algonquian Indian Words (New England)*, 1996. This book is a dictionary of roots, words, phrases and sentences, and grammar with examples. Our Internet Website contains additional information (O'Brien, 2005).

Appendix V discusses the language project, and Appendix VI gives an extensive Pronunciation Guide to the language.

---

4. We would like to mention the generosity of Mary Benjamin who allowed us to quote from her audio recording of Princess Red Wings' words. Mary Benjamin's forthcoming book, *The Memoirs of Princess Red Wing*, will be of interest to many readers.

ENDNOTES

1. Only minor changes have been made to the 16th and 17th century documents. The changes were made to improve readability. For example, writers wrote a long "f" like—*f*—for our modern day "s"; we changed *f* to read "s" for obvious reasons. Occasionally we insert brackets [ ] into the original quotes to provide clarifying information with regard to spelling, word meaning or interpretation of facts. Overall, the spelling, word meanings and grammar of the original documents are preserved in their original form. The reader should also know that when reading old documents you will see the word y^e (not the same as "ye" meaning "you"); ye means "the." Also, when you see y^t, it means "that".

2. The method of recording time in the 1500s and 1600s was different from the way our calendar works today. Our calendar calls the first day of the year "January 1" and last day of the year "December 31". In the 1500s and 1600s the method of recording time was in the so-called Old Style (abbreviated O.S.), and based on the Julian Calendar. In the Old Style, the first day of the new year was March 25 [the Spring or Vernal Equinox (some use March 21 since there were two "official" versions throughout European history)]. In writings from the period, March is called the first month, April is called the second month, etc. The last month of the year was February.

   Note, in the next section all dates are in this Old Style. Thus, when you see an old date from the 1500s and 1600s, knock off about two months to get the modern time of year. Use the following tables to convert months and years from Old Style to New Style (our modern time) [for *days*, add 11 to day given].

Month Differences

Month	Old Style (1500s and 1600s)	New Style (Modern)
1st month	March	January
2nd month	April	February
3rd month	May	March
4th month	June	April
5th month	July	May
6th month	August	June
7th month	September	July
8th month	October	August
9th month	November	September
10th month	December	October
11th month	January	November
12th month	February	December

Example of Year Differences Seen in Records (Years Differ Between Jan 1 - 24 Mar.)

Month	Old Style	New Style
January	1675	1676 [New Year, Jan. 1]
February	1675	1676
March	1676 [New Year, March 25]	1676
April	1676	1676
March	1676	1676
June	1676	1676
July	1676	1676
August	1676	1676
September	1676	1676
October	1676	1676
November	1676	1676
December	1676	1676
January	1676	1677 [New Year, Jan. 1]
February	1676	1677
March	1677 [New Year, Mar. 25]	1677

For example, in Gookin (1674), the missionary Richard Bourne at Sandwich, Cape Cod, signs a letter to his boss Gookin, as "1. of the 7 month, 1674", meaning "July 21st" in our time and "September 1" in their time. For more information see *Harvard Guide to American History,* Handlin (1955).

3. This book contains 7 appendices at the end of the book. They are included to suit the interests of different readers. See Table of Contents for page numbers.

4. There is an interesting and common fallacy of reasoning we seem to find among some modern historians and anthropologists who write books and journal articles about "the Indians". Such scholars are committed to the "scientific method" in judging "data" from different sources—such as ground excavations, historical documents, interviews with Native peoples, and others. The fallacy of reasoning we are talking about can be summarized like this:

> "If I look for something but don't find it, I assume it doesn't exist." This is a reasonable view if we are talking about a court of law. If a suspect cannot provide corroborating evidence to substantiate an alibi, courts assume the alibi is bogus.

To show the fallacy, let's state the fallacy in symbolic terms using mathematical logic. Let F mean "I found something". Let E mean "it exists". Then, in propositional calculus

$$[(F \supset E) \cdot \neg F] \supset \neg E \qquad [1]$$

where the symbols have standard meanings (Purtill, 1971). To give example of this fallacy, let's say you loose your car keys one afternoon. You think your keys might be at a local library you visited. You look "high-and-low" but fail to find them. You say "they are not at the library". But, they could be there! Maybe you just didn't look exactly where they are in the library. This is clearly invalid reasoning meaning it is illogical or incorrect.

A better approach would be to say, "It may exist or it may not exist, even if I looked but didn't find it". Again, symbolically

$$[(F \supset E) \cdot \neg F] \supset E \vee \neg E \qquad [2]$$

From Equation [2], we could say "Now, I didn't find my keys at the library, so maybe I didn't loose my keys at the library, but maybe I did."

The type of false reasoning (in Equation [1]) is seen when local anthropologists belittle or deny the use or validity of oral tradition. This pervasive fallacy of formal reasoning tends to color the attitudes of people, further perpetuating stereotypes and racialism, thereby denying the tenets of our democratic form of government. We pray that our best scholars not fall prey to the lions of irrationality. We hope they will attend more to the essential forms of logical thought which is their scientific tradition.

Scholars should realize that being elected to the National Academy of Arts or Sciences is not the highest recognition in the eyes of everyone.

5. Some scholars write that the Massachusett language is "extinct" (like dinosaurs, the dodo birds and hundreds of other living things). Let's explain why this is not possible. Our language never died because it is the voice of Mother Earth. The language is in all of her songs. When you hear the dignified and beautiful Canadian goose say *hònck* he is singing his song. When the majestic lightening cracks and you hear *cutshâusha*, he talks the talk. When we see the skilled artist pounding out her metal we hear the *togwonck* of her pounding. When the Snow Spirit covers the sky with soft clouds of snow, we hear *muhpoo*, and Mother Earth sings once again. The Great Spirit gave us so many sounds in the language which are in nature, we can never forget them. Do you think the Great Spirit would give us our language only for a little while—until the Superior White Man would come, and everything died? This contradicts all metaphysical truths self-evident to all of God's Children.

So you see, our language never died in the first place! We should pray for scholars for whom life seems so hard.

CULTURAL OBSERVATIONS ARRANGED BY TOPIC

THEIR APPEARANCE

The First Known Written Description of the Wampanoag [Narragansett?] in Newport, RI by Italian Explorer Giovanni da Verrazzano [June, 1524?]

We proceeded [from Block Island] to another place, fifteen leagues [about 45 miles] distant from the island, where we found a very excellent harbor [Newport, RI]. Before entering it, we saw about twenty small boats of people, who came about our ship, uttering many cries of astonishment, but they would not approach nearer than within fifty paces; stopping, they looked at the structure of our ship, our persons and dress, afterwards they all raised a loud shout together, signifying that they were pleased. By imitating their signs, we inspired them in some measure with confidence, so that they came near enough for us to toss to them some little bells and glasses, and many toys, which they took and looked at, laughing. and then came on board without fear.

Among them were two kings more beautiful in form and stature than can possibly be described; one was about forty years, the other about twenty four, and they were dressed in the following manner: The oldest had a deer's skin around his body, artificially wrought in damask figures, his head was without covering, his hair was tied back in various knots; around his neck he wore a large chain ornamented with many stones of different colors. The young man was similar in his general appearance. This is the finest looking tribe, and the handsomest in their costumes, that we have found in our voyage. They exceeded us in size, and they are of a very fair complexion; some of them incline to white, and others to a tawny colour; their faces are sharp, their hair long and black, upon the adorning of which they bestow great pains; their eyes are black and sharp, their expressions mild and pleasant, greatly resembling the antique.

I say nothing [in modesty] to the other parts of the body, which are all in good proportion, and such as belong to well-formed men. Their women are of the same form and beauty, very graceful of fine countenances and pleasing appearance in manners and modesty; they wear no clothing except a deer skin, ornamented like those worn by the men; some wear very rich lynx skins upon their arms, and various ornaments upon their heads, composed of braids of hair, which also hang down upon their breasts on each side. Others wear different ornaments, such as the women of Egypt and Syria use. The older and married people, both men and women, wear many ornaments in their ears, hanging down in the oriental manner.

We saw upon them several pieces of wrought copper, which is more esteemed by them than gold, as this is of value on account of its colour, but is considered by them as the most ordinary of the metals—yellow being the colour especially disliked by them; azure and red are those in the highest estimation with them. Of these things which we gave then, they prized most highly the bells, azure crystals, and other toys to hang in their ears and about their necks; they do not value or care to have silk or gold stuffs, or other kinds of cloth, not implements of steel or iron.

When we showed them our arms [weapons] they expressed no admiration, and only asked how they were made; the same was the case with the looking-glasses, which they returned to us, smiling as soon as they had looked at them. They are very generous, giving away whatever they have.

We formed a great friendship with them, and one day we entered the port with out ship, having before rode at the distance of a league from the shore, as the weather was adverse. They came off to the ship with a number of little boats, with their faces painted in divers colours, showing us real signs of joy, bringing us of their provisions, and signifying to us where we could best ride in safety with our ship, and keeping with us until we had cast anchor. We remained among them fifteen days, to provide ourselves with many things of which we were in want, during which time they came every day to see our ship, bringing with them their wives of whom they were very careful; for, although they came on board themselves, and remained a long while, they made their wives stay in the boats, nor could we ever get them on board by any entreaties or at presents we could make them.

One of the two kings often came with his queen and many attendants, to see us for his amusement; but he always stopped at the distance of about two hundred paces, and sent a boat to inform us of his intended visit, saying they would come and see our ship—this was done for safety, and as soon as they had an answer from us they came off, and remained awhile to look around; but on hearing the annoying cries of the sailors, the king sent the queen, with her attendants, in a very light boat, to wait, near an island a quarter of a league distant from us, while he remained a long time on board, talking with us by signs, and expressing his fanciful notions about every things in the ship, and asking the use of all.

After imitating our modes of salutation, and tasting our food, he courteously took leave of us. Sometimes, when our men stayed two or three days on a small island, near the ship, for their necessities [drink and sex], as sailors are wont to do, he came with seven or eight of his attendants, to inquire about our movements, often asking us if we intended to remain there long, and offering us everything at his command, and then he would shoot with his bow, and run up and down with his people, making great sport for us.

We often went five or six leagues into the interior, and found the country as pleasant as is possible to conceive, adapted to cultivation of every kind, whether of corn, wine or oil; there are open plains twenty-five or thirty leagues in extent, entirely free from trees or other hindrances, and as great fertility, that whatever is sown will yield an excellent crop. On entering the woods, we observed that they might all be traversed by an army ever so numerous; the trees of which were composed, were oaks, cypresses, and other unknown in Europe. We found, also, apples, plumbs, filberts, and many other fruits, but all of a different kind from ours. (from *The Voyages of Giovanni da Verrazzano, 1524-1528*; quoted in Lenz, 1994, pp. 27-30)

General Appearance of Native Peoples in Southeastern New England

[Of] their stature, most of them are between five or six foot high, straight bodied, strongly composed, smooth-skinned, merry countenanced, of complexion something more swarthy than Spaniards, black haired, high foreheaded, black eyed, out-nosed, broad shouldered, brawny armed, long and slender handed, out breasted, small waisted, lank bellied, well thighed, flat kneed, handsome grown legs, and small feet. In a word, take them when the blood brisks in their veins, when the flesh is on their backs, when they frolic in their antic deportments and Indian postures, and they are more amiable to behold than many a compounded fantastic in the newest fashion.

It may puzzle belief to conceive such lusty bodies should have their rise and daily supportment from so slender a fostering, their houses being mean, their lodging as homely, commons scant, their drink water, and nature their best clothing. In them the old proverb may well be verified: *Natura paucis contenta* [Nature is satisfied with few things].

I have been in many places, yet did I never see one that was born either in redundance or defect a monster, or any that sickness had deformed, or causally made decrepit, saving one that had a bleared eye and another that had a wen on his cheek. The reason is rendered why they grow so proportionable and continue so long in their vigor (most of them being fifty before a wrinkled brow or gray hair betray their age) is because they are not brought down with suppressing labor, vexed with annoying cares, or drowned in excessive abuse of overflowing plenty, which oftentimes kills them more than want, as may appear in them. For when they change their bare Indian commons for the plenty of England's full diet, it is so contrary to their stomachs that death is or a desperate sickness immediately accrues, which makes so few of them desirous of seeing England. (Wm. Wood, 1634; quoted in Lenz, 1995b, pp. 67-68)

They Live Long

They live long, even to an hundred years of age, if they not be cut off by the Children, war or the [European-brought] plague. (John Josselyn, *An Account of two Voyages to New-England*, 1675; quoted in Lenz, 1995c, p. 194)

They .... lived long lives. I have seen Indians of a hundred and twenty and forty years of age who still went to hunt the moose. (Nicholas Denys, 1672; quoted in Lenz, 1995c, p. 143)

... they are not of a dumpish, sad nature, but rather naturally cheerful.... (Wm. Wood, 1634; quoted in Lenz, 1995b, p. 76)

They used to oil their skins and hair with bear's grease heretofore, but now with swine's fat, and then paint their faces with vermilion, or other red, and powder their heads. Also they use black and white paints; and make one part of their face of one colour; and another, of another, very deformedly. The women especially do thus; some men also, especially when they are marching to their wars; and hereby, as they think, are more terrible to their enemies. (Gookin, 1674, p. 13)

Wampanoag Massasoit Ousa Mequin First Meets the Pilgrims [Sunday, March 18, 1621]

On this day came again the savage [meaning Samoset of the Maine Abenaki—the first to meet English] and brought with him five other tall proper [sturdy] men. They had, every man, a deer's skin on him and the principal of them [Massasoit] had a wild cat's akin or such on the one arm. They had, most of them long hosen [leggings] up to their groins close made; and above their groins to their waist, another leather.... They are of complexion like our English Gypsies. No hair, or very little, on their faces. On their heads, long hair to the shoulders; only cut before: some tussed up before with a feather, broadwise like a fan' another [with a] fox's tail hanging out. (from *Mourt's Relation*; quoted in Lenz, 1995a, p. 38)

Appearance of the Massasoit Ousa Mequin

In His appearance he [the Massasoit] is a very lusty [strong] man, in his best years, [of] an able body, grave of countenance, and spare of speech. In his attire, [he was] little or nothing different from the rest of his followers only in a great chain of white bone berads [beads?] around his neck, hangs a little bag of tobacco which he drank [smoked] and gave us to drink [smoke]. His face was painted with a sad [deep] red like murrey [mulberry color] and [he] oiled both head and face [so] that he looked greasily. All his followers likewise were, in their faces, in part or in whole, painted: some black, some red, some yellow and some white; some with crosses and other antic [odd or fantastic] works. Some had skins on them and some naked: all strong, all [real] men in appearance. (from *Mourt's Relation*; quoted in Lenz, 1995a, p. 41)

GREETING AND LANGUAGE

I cannot observe that they ever had (before the comming of the *English* or *French* or *Dutch* amongst them) any *Names* to difference *themselves* from strangers, for they knew none .... [T]wo sorts of *names* they had, and have amongst *themselves*. First, *generall*, belonging, to all *Natives*, as *Nínnuock, Ninnimissinnûwock, Eniskeetompaûwog,* which signifies *Men, Folke, or People.* Second, particuar names, peculiar to severall Nations, of them amongst *Themselves,as, Nanhiggan̂euck, Massacus̃euck, Cawasums̃euck, Cowwes̃euck, Quintikóock, Qunnipi̢euck, Pequttóog, etc.* (Roger Williams, *Introduction*, 1643)

They often ask mee why wee [English] call them *Indians, Natives, &c.* and understanding the reason, they will call themselves *Indians,* in opposition to *English,* &c. (Roger Williams, *Introduction*, 1643)

A Single Language with Dialects was Spoken Throughout Region

There is a mixture of this *Language North* and *South,* [and] within two hundred miles ... their *Dialects* doe exceedingly differ; yet not so [much] ... a man may ... converse with *thousands* of *Natives* all over the *Countrey.* (Roger Williams, *Introduction*, 1643)

.... [Others] (and my selfe) have conceived some of their words to have Affinitie [be like] with the Hebrew.... I have found a greater Affinitie of their Language with the *Greek* Tongue. (Roger Williams,

Introduction, 1643)

The Indians of the parts of New England, especially upon the sea coasts, use the same sort of language, only with some differences in the expressions, as they differ in several countries [counties?] in England yet so as they can well understand one another. Their speech is a distinct speech from any of the those used in Europe, Asia, or Africa, that I ever heard. (Daniel Gookin, 1674, p. 9)

Their language is hard to learn, few of the English being able to speak any of it, or capable of right pronunciation, which is the chief grace of their tongue.... They love any man that can utter his mind in their words. (William Wood, 1634; quoted in Lenz, 1995b, p. 86)

    As for the [Wampanoag] langauge it is very copious, large and difficult. As yet [Sept. 10, 1623] we cannot attain to any great measure thereof: but can understand them and explain ourselves to their understanding; by the help of those that daily converse with us. And though there be [a] difference in a hundred miles distance of place both in language and manners, yet [it is] not so much but that they very well understand each other
    And thus much of their lives and manners. (Edward Winslow, 1624; quoted in Lenz, 1995b, p. 11)

Wunnêtu Nittà <> *My Heart is Good*

This speech they use when ever they professe their honestie; they naturally confessing that all goodnesse is first in the heart. (Roger Williams, 1643)

Massachusett Language: One of the Longest Words Ever Recorded in New England Indian Languages.

nup-pahk-nuh-tô-pe-pe-nau-wut-chut-chuh-quô-ka-neh-cha-neh-cha-e-nin-nu-mun-nô-nōk

Translation: "Our well-skilled looking-glass makers." (Trumbull, 1903)

What cheare Nétop? *is the general salutation of all English toward them.* Nétop *is friend.* (Roger Williams, 1643)

From these courteous *Salutations* Observe in general: There is a savour of *civility* and *courtesie* even amongst these wild *Americans*, both amongst *themselves* and towards *strangers*. (Roger Williams, 1643)

Naming the Children (Long Island)

They use to make great dances.... They make great preparations for these dances, of wampum, beads, jewels, dishes, and clothing, and liquors, &c. Sometimes two or three families join in naming their children.... When they have got all things ready, they will call their neighbors together, very often send to other towns of Indians, and when they have all got together, they will begin their dance, and to distribute the gifts, and every person that receives the gifts or liquors, gets up and pronounces the name that a child is to be called by, with a loud voice three times. But sometimes a young man or woman will be ashamed to pronounce the name, and they will get some other person to do it. Very often one family will make small preparations, and call few old people to name a child; and it was common with them to name their children two or three times over by different names, and at different times, and old people very often gave new names to themselves. (Samson Occum, 1809; quoted in Simmons, 1986, pp. 46-47)

Their Personal Names They Change Throughout Life

All their names are significant and variable for when they come to the state of men and women [and at marriage] they alter them according to their deeds and dispositions. (Winslow, 1624; quoted in Lenz, 1995b, p. 10)

Obscure and meane persons amongst them have no Names.... Againe, because they abhorre to name the dead (Death being the

King of Terrours to all naturall men): and though the Natives hold the Soule to live ever.... In that respect I say, if any of their *Sáchims* or neighbors die who were of their names, they lay down those Names as dead. (Roger Williams, 1643)

... seldom are their words and their deeds strangers.... (Wm. Wood, 1634; quoted in Lenz, 1995b, p. 86)

Massachusett Language: Conversational Lesson
Greeting of the Day Lesson

Mah-tomp-an woo-nee
Good Morning

Tah ku-teen-uk-kee-te-am?
How Are You?

Woo-nik-kee-tee-am taû-bot-nee
Fine, Thank You

Kah keen?
And You?

Moo-tá-ee woo-nee
Very Good

Ke-suk woo-neeg-in
It Is A Beautiful Day

Nux woo-nee-noo-á-onk
Yes, I Agree (Good Talk)

Pah-shee-quá-ee-you ah-quom-pee
It's Noon Time

Ah-quam-pee nee-woot-chee meet-soo-onk
It Is Time To Eat

Qoo-took-quaw-quaw woo-nee
Good Afternoon

Mat koo-nun-o-us nee-woot-chee pah-suk nah-ad-took
I haven't Seen You For A Long Time

Tah woo-teeg-in?
Where Keep You?

Noo-tay-ee ut on-kah-ak oo-tan-nee-mees
I Dwell In Another Village

Woo-nan-quay-ee woo-nee
Good Evening

Noo-kan woo-nee-gin
It Is A Beautiful Night

Ah-nock-sook mah-nah-tash
There Are Many Stars

Kah nux pah-kok
And Yes, Clear Skies

Mat pah-sook mah-tooks
Not One Cloud

Kah pah-sook ah-koo-mus nee-pahz-shad woo-neeg-in
And A Beautiful Grand Mother Moon

A-quee-nee kah nah-han-noosh-shak
Peace And Farewell

Nahck-oos-kor-at-tit-ee-ah wonk tee-an-uk
Let Us Meet Again Soon

Ah-poo nan-au-an-tam-oo-ee
Remain Careful (Take Care)
Pad-char
Until (In Departing Of A Friend)
From Moondancer and Strong Woman, *Understanding Algonquian Indian Words* (New England), 1996. Lesson adapted from teachings of Chief Spotted Eagle of the Nipmuck Nation at the Algonquin Indian School, Rhode Island Indian Council.

Nunnooham Wutche Ahki

aa oooo	psuk	togkonk	s - s - k
sésikw	ptoowu	popow	- sk -
pussoúgh	kaukont	tawk	s - k
pootau	hònck	keeshk	- s - sk -
nkèke	hónckock	mskik	'sh
sickíssuog	wushówunan	muhpoo	t - q
poopohs	oohoo	sóchepo	ts - p
	choochoo	cutshausha	q - p
	pahpahsa	paashk	'pe
	kukkow	quequan	sq

Title: I Sing for Mother Earth

The words in the poem are a selection of sounds of land animals, water animals, sky animals, human animals, nature, and "pure sounds." The sounds are derived from historical sources and linguistic reconstruction.

EATING AND ENTERTAINMENT

Whomever commeth in when they are eating, they offer them to eat of that which they are eating, they offer them to eat of that which they have, though but little enough prepar'd for themselves. If any provision of *fish* or *flesh* come in, they make their neighbors partakers with them.
    If any stranger come in, they presently give him to eate of what they have; many a time, and at all times of the night (as I have fallen in travell upon their houses) when nothing hath been ready, have themselves and their wives, risen to prepare me some refreshing. (Roger Williams, 1643)

It is a strange *truth*, that a man shall find more free entertainment and refreshing amongst these Barbarians then amongst thousands that call themselves *Christians*. (Roger Williams, 1643)

They are much given to hospitality in their way. If any stranger come to their houses, they will give him the best lodgings and diet they have; and by her husband's direction, delivers to the strangers, according to their quality, or his affection. (Gookin, 1674, p. 13)

Their food is generally boiled maize, or Indian corn, mixed with kidney beans, or sometimes without. Also they frequently boil in this pottage fish, either new or dried, as shads, eels, alewives or a kind of herring, or any other sort of fish.... Also they boil in this furmenty all sorts of flesh, they take in hunting; as venison, beaver, bear's flesh, moose, otters, rackoons, or any kind that they take in hunting. Also they mix with the said pottage several sorts of roots; as Jerusale artichokes, and ground sorts, and other roots, and pompions, and squashes and also several sorts of nuts or masts, as oak-acorns, chesnuts, walnuts: these husked and dried, and powered, they thicken their pottage therewith. Also sometimes they beat their maize into meal, and sift it through a basket, made for that purpose. With this meal they make bread, baking it in the ashes, covering the dough with leaves. Sometimes they make a meal of their meal a small sort of cakes, and boil them. They also make a certain sort of meal of parched maize. This meal they call nokake. It is so sweet, toothsome and hearty, that an Indian will travel many days with no other food but this meal, which he eateth as he needs, and after drinketh water. And for this end, when they travel a journey, or go a hunting, they carry this nokake in a basket, or bag, for their use. (Gookin, 1674, pp. 10-11)

When they visit our English, being invited to eat, they are very moderate... but at home they will eat till their bellies stand south [are full] to eat at some times and sometimes nothing at all. [William Wood, 1634; quoted in Lenz, 1995b, p. 71)

Pure Water is all They Drink

Their natural drinke is of the Cristall fountain [pure water] and this they take up in their hands by joyning [them] close together. They take up a great quantity at a time, and drink at the wrists. (Thomas Morton, 1632; quoted in Lenz, 1995b, p. 57)

Alcohol — The Destroyer of Indians was Brought by Europeans

Their drink was formerly no other than water, and yet it doth continue, for their general and common drink. Many of the Indians are lovers of strong drink [alcohol].... Hereby they are made drunk very often; and being drunk, are many times outrageous & mad, fighting with and killing one another; yea sometimes their own relatives.

This beastly sin of drunkenness could not be charged upon the Indians before the English and other Christians nations... came to dwell in America. (Gookin, 1674, p. 11)

The Indians were the first to make maple syrup and sugar, and today the original process is still used commercially. (Princess Red Wing, in Kaiser, p. 8)

SLEEPING AND LODGING

More from Voyages of Italian Explorer Giovanni da Verrazzano, Newport, RI

We saw their dwellings, which are of a circular form, of about ten or twelve paces in circumference, made of logs split in halves, without any regularity of architecture, and covered with roofs of straw, nicely put on, which protect them from wind and rain. There is no doubt that they could build stately edifices if they had workmen a skilful as ours, for the whole sea-coast abounds in shining stones, crystals, and alabaster, and for the same reason it has coverts and retreats for animals.

They change their habitations from place to place as circumstances of situation and season may require; this is easily done, as they only take with them their mats, and they have their houses [elsewhere] prepared already. The father and whole family dwell together in one house in great numbers; in some we saw twenty-five or thirty persons. (from *The Voyages of Giovanni da Verrazzano, 1524-1528*; quoted in Lenz, 1994, p. 31)

The Natives of New England are accustomed to build their houses like the Wild Irish. (Thomas Morton, 1632; quoted in Lenz, 1995b, p. 42)

Their houses, or wigwams, are built with small poles fixed in the ground, bent and fastened together with barks of trees oval or arbour-wife on the top. The best sort of their houses are covered very neatly tight, and warm, with barks of trees, stripped from their bodies, as such seasons when the sap is up; and made into great flakes with pressures of weighty timber; when they are green; and so becoming dry, they will retain a form suitable for the use they prepare them for. The meaner sort of wigwams are covered with mats, they make of a kind of bulrush, which they also indifferent tight and warm, but not so good as the former. These houses they make of several sizes, according to their activity and ability; some twenty, some forty feet long, and broad. Some I have seen of sixty or a hundred feet long, and thirty feet broad. In the smaller sort, they make a fire in the centre of the house; and have a lower hole on the top of the house, to let out the smoke. They keep the door into the wigwams always shut, by a mat falling thereon, as people go in and out. This they do to prevent air coming in, which will cause much smoke in very windy weather. If the smoke beat down at the lower hole, they hang a little mat, in the way of a screen, on the top of the house, which they can with a cord turn to the windward side, which prevents the smoke. In the greater houses they make two, three or four fires, at a distance one from another, for the better accommodation of the people belonging to it. I have often lodged in their wigwams; and have found them as warm as the best English houses. In their wigwams, they make a kind of couch or mattress, firm and strong raised about a foot high from the earth; first covered with boards that they split out of trees; and upon the boards they spread mats generally, and sometimes bear skins and deer skins. These are large enough for three or four persons to lodge upon; and one may draw nearer, or keep at a distance from the heat of the fire, as they please; for their mattresses are six or eight feet broad. (Gookin, 1674, p. 10)

[Their wigwams] are warmer then our English houses. (Wm. Wood, 1634; quoted in Lenz, 1995b, p. 87)

People So Happy They Sing Together as They Fall Off to Sleep

...the savages'... sing themselves asleep. (*Mourt's Relation*, 1622; quoted in Lenz, 1995a, p. 47)

I Will Sleep Without Doors

Which I have knowne them contentedly doe, by a fire under a tree, when sometimes some *English* have (for want of familiaritie and language with them) been fearefull to entertaine them.

In Summer-time I have knowne them lye abroad often themselves, to make roome for strangers, *English*, or other. (Roger Williams, 1643)

Let Us Lay on Wood

This they doe plentifully when they lie down to sleep winter and summer, abundance they have, and abundance they lay on: their Fire is instead of our bedcloaths. And so, themselves and any that have occasion to lodge with them, must be content to turne often to the Fire, if the night be cold, and they who first awake must repair the Fire. (Roger Williams, 1643)

When they have a bad Dreame, which they conceive to be a threatening from God, they fall to prayer at all times of the night, especially early before day.... (Roger Williams, 1643)

NUMBERS

From the first missionary grammar book [1666] on Massachusett language:
(∞ = oo as in "food")

Numerals belong unto *Adnouns* [adjectives] and in them there is something remarkable. From the Number 5 and upward, they *adde a word suppletive*, which signifieth nothing, but receiveth the Grammatical variation of the *Declension*, according to the *things* numbered, *Animate* or *Inanimate*. The *Additional* is (*tohsú*) or (*tahshé*) which is varied (*tohsúog, tohsúash,* or *tohshinash*).

For Example:

1 *Nequt.*
2 *Neese.*
3 *Nish.*
4 *Yau.*
5 *Napanna tahshe* { ohsuog. / ohsuash.

6 *Nequtta tahshe.*
7 *Nesausuk tahshe.*
8 *Shwosuk tahshe.*
9 *Pask∞gun tahshe.*
10 *Piuk. Piukqussuog, piukqussuash.*

As for Example:

Then from 10 to 20 they *adde* afore the numeral (*nab* or *nabo*) and then it is not needful to *adde the following additional*, though sometimes they do it.

11 *Nabo Nequt.*	16 *Nabo Nequtta.*
12 *Nabo Neese.*	17 *Nabo Nesausuk.*
13 *Nabo Nish.*	18 *Nabo Shwosuk.*
14 *Nabo Yau.*	19 *Nabo Pask?gun.*
15 *Nabo Napanna.*	20 *Neesneechag* { kodtog. / kodtash.

Then *upwards* they *adde* to *Neesneechag*, the *single Numbers* to 30 and so forth.

30   *Nishwinchag kodtog, kodtash.*
40   *Yauunchag kodtog, kodtash.*
50   *Napanna tahshinchag kodtog, kodtash.*
60   *Nequtta tahshinchag kodtog, kodtash.*
70   *Nesausuk tahshinchag kodtog, kodtash.*
80   *Shwosuk tahshinchag kodtog, kodtash.*
90   *Pask∞gun tahshinchag kodtog, kodtash*
100   *Nequt pasuk k∞og. k∞ash.*
1000 *Nequt muttannonganog* { kodtog. / kodtash. } *or* { kussuog. / kussuash.

(John Eliot, 1666)

Napanna tashe tohsuog anumwog = "25 dogs." (Strong Woman and Moondancer, *A Massachusett Language Book, Vol. 1.*, 1998)

Nquit pausuckóemittànnug   100000

Having no Letters nor Arts, 'tis admirable how quick they are in casting up great numbers, with the helpe of graines of Corne, instead of *Europes* pens or counters. (Roger Williams, 1643)

[*AUTHOR'S NOTE*—We know very little about the accomplishments of our ancestors in mathematics, astronomy, meteorology, botany, pharmacology, and so forth. Like other First Indigenous Peoples of America, the Wampanoag and other Algonquian-speaking peoples of our region must have been keen observers of the Laws of Nature for their very survival depended on being able to read the stars, the winds, clouds, the leafs, and all of the Great Spirit's signs and omens.]

FAMILY AND RELATIONS

Indian Laws Were Very Simple

The law which they observed in old times was this—to do to another only that which they wished to be done to them. All lived in good friendship & understanding. They refused no thing to one another. If one wigwam or family had not provisions enough, the neighbors supplied them, although they had only that which was necessary for themselves. And in all things it was the same. They lived pure lives; their wives were faithful to their husbands, and the girls were chaste. (Nicholas Denys, *The Description & Natural History of the Coasts of New England*, 1672; quoted in Lenz, 1995c, p. 155)

Such is their love for one another that they cannot endure to see their countrymen wronged, but will stand stiffly in their defense, plead strongly in their behalf, and justify one another's integrities in any warrantable action. (Wm. Wood, 1634; quoted in Lenz, 1995b, p. 74)

Such is their mild temper of their spirits that they cannot endure objurgations or scolding... I have been among diverse of them, yet did I never see any falling out amongst them, not so much as cross words or reviling speeches which might provoke to blows. (Wm. Wood, 1634; quoted in Lenz, 1995b, p. 76)

They hold the band of brother-hood so deare, that when one had commited a murther and fled, they executed his brother; and 'tis common for a brother to pay the debt of a brother deceased. (Roger Williams, 1643)

There are no beggars amongst them, nor fatherlesse children unprovided for. (Roger Williams, 1643)

Strong Love of Their Children Which the English Frowned Upon and Made Them Change

Their *affections*, especially to their children, are very strong; so that I have knowne a *Father* take so grievously the losse of his *childe*, that he hath cut and stob'd himselfe with *griefe* and *rage*. (Roger Williams, 1643)

They love their children greatly. (Nicholas Denys, 1672; quoted in Lenz, 1995c, p. 146.)

The Rite of Passage for Young Boys

When there is a youth who begins to approach manhood, he is taken by his father, uncle, or nearest friend, and he is conducted blindfolded into a wilderness, in order that he may not know the way, and he is left there by night or otherwise, with a bow and arrows, and hatchet and a knife. He must support himself there a whole winter with what the scanty earth furnishes at this season, and by hunting. Towards the spring they come again, and fetch him out of it... until May. He must then go out again every morning with the person who is ordered to take him... to seek wild herbs and roots, which they know to be the most poisonous and bitter... which he must drink.... And if he cannot retain it, he must repeat the dose until he can support it. (Issack de Rasieres, about 1628; quoted in Simmons, 1986, p. 47)

Being a Man

A man is not accounted a man till he do some notable act or shew forth such courage and resolution as becometh his place. (Winslow,

1624; quoted in Lenz, 1995b, p. 18)

All Elders Were Respected

The younger sort reverence the elder and do all mean offenses whilst they are together [even] although they be strangers [to each other]. (Edward Winslow, 1624; quoted in Lenz, 1995b, p. 10)

Modern Reverence for Elders

The Elders

Kehchisog

The Elders	Kehchisog
The Elders pray for the rising of the sun	Kehchisog peantamwog wutche pashpishont
The Elders pray for the setting of the sun	Kehchisog peantamwog wutche wayont
We pray for the Elders	Nuppeantamumun wutche Kehchisog
"Elders, please pray for the rising of the sun"	"Kechisog nissimun peantam∞k wutche pashpishont"
"Elders, please pray for the setting of the sun"	"Kechchisog nissimun peantam∞k wutche wayont"
The sun rises	Nepáuz pashpishau
The sun sets	Wayau

(Strong Woman and Moondancer, *A Massachusett Language Book, Vol. 1*, 1998)

Give Aways—An Old Custom [see Religion, also]

They delight very much in their dancings and revelings; at which time he that danceth... will give away in his frolick all that he hath, gradually some to one, and some to another, according to his fancy and affection. And then... another [person] succeeds and doth the like; so successively, one after another, night after night [they do this give away ceremony]... which are mostly at their harvests. (Gookin, 1674; quoted in Lenz, 1995c, p. 206)

DOMESTIC

Commonly they never shut their doores, day nor night; and 'tis rare that any hurt is done. (Roger Williams, 1643)

... women and maids live apart in, foure, five, or six dayes, in the time of their monethly sicknesse, which custome in all parts of the Countrey they strictly observe, and no *Male* may come into that house. (Roger Williams, 1643)

They are full of businesse, and as impatient of hinderance (in their kind) as any Merchant in *Europe*. (Roger Williams, 1643)

Of their several arts and employments, at first in dressing all manner of skins, which they do by scraping and rubbing, afterwards painting them with antic embroiderings in unchangaeble colors.... Their bows they make of a handsome shape, strung commonly with the sinews of mooses; their arrows are made of young eldern, feathered with feathers of eagles' wings and tails, headed with brass in shape of a heart or triangle, fastened in a slender piece of wood six or seven inches long which is framed to put loose in the pithy eldern that is bound for riving. (Wm. Wood, 1634; quoted in Lenz, 1995b, p. 85)

Their women constantly beat all their corne with hand: they plant it, dresse it, gather it, barne it, beat it, and take as much paines as any people in the world, which labour is questionlesse one cause of their extraordinary ease of childbirth. (Roger Williams, 1643)

It is almost incredible what burthens the poore women carry of *Corne*, of *Fish*, of *Beanes*, of *Mats*, and a childe besides. (Roger Williams, 1643)

... Indian women... are quickly and easily delivered and many times are so strong, not within a few hours after the child's birth, they will go about their ordinary occasions [back on their feet again]. (Gookin, 1674, p. 15)

Their Children—General New England Customs

Their infants are borne with hair on their heads and are of a complexion white as our nation [English], but their mothers in their infancy make a bath of Wallnut leaves, huskes of Walnuts [sic] and such things as will staine their skin for ever, wherein they dip and washe them to make them tawny. (Thomas Morton, 1632, quoted in Lenz, 1995b, p. 45)

When their children are borne they bind them up on a piece of board, and sets it upright, either against a tree or any other place. They keep them thus bound untill they are be three months old, and after the are continuall naked until they be about five or six years. You shall have [see] them many times take their Children & bury them in the snow all but their faces for a time, to make the better to endure cold, and when they are not about 2, years old, the will take them and cast them into the Sea, like a little dogge or Cat, to learn them to swimme.... (quoted in Lenz, 1995a, p. 94)

Their Music is Lullabies

For their carriage it is very civil, smiles being their greatest grace of their mirth; their music is lullabies to quit their children, who generally are as quiet as if they had neither spleen or lungs. To hear one of these Indians unseen, a good ear might easily mistake their untaught voice for the warbling of a well-tuned instrument, such command have they of their voice. (Wm. Wood, 1634; quoted in Lenz, 1995b, p. 67)

How the Song—Rock-A-Bye-Baby—Started

Your mothers might have sung "rock-a bye-baby-on-the-tree-top," but it was the little Indian babies on their cradle boards who rocked on the tree tops.

The Indian woman were getting ready for their Strawberry Thanksgiving over in Plymouth and hung their babies on the trees all around the fields while they were picking wild strawberries for their feast. Then they put one young Indian to watch.

And while he was watching, he began singing a song and whittling a stick. By and by a Pilgrim man sat down beside him. The Indian, he kept right on singing, kept right on whittling. By and by the Pilgrim man nudged him and said, "I like your song, I like your song" as he pointed to his lips. By and by the Indian understood what he was talking about and said, "Wind rock baby, but by and by wind blow fast, bough break, down come babies' cradle and all." And he laughed when he thought what a squall it would be if they all came tumbling down at once.

Well, the Pilgrim man smiled too, but he took a piece of birch bark and wrote it out—

> Rock-a-bye-baby-in-the-tree-top, when the wind blows the cradle will rock. When the bow breaks the cradle will fall, and down will come baby cradle and all.

And he took it down to his Pilgrim mothers, and they have been singing it to their babies ever since.

So you see, it wasn't you who rocked on the tree top. It was the little Indian babies on their cradle boards that rocked on the tree top. (traditional; recorded in Princess Red Wing, 1986)

Whence they call *English-men* Chauquaquock, that is, *knive-men*, stone formerly being to them in stead of *Knives, Awle-blades, Hatchets* and *Howes*. (Roger Williams, 1643)

Many of them naturally Princes, or else industrious persons, are rich; and the poore amongst them will say, they want nothing. (Roger Williams, 1643)

... generally all the men throughout the Countrey have a *Tobacco-bag* with a *pipe* in it, hanging at their back: sometimes they make such great *pipes*, both of *wood* and *stone*, that they are two feet long, with men or beasts carved, so big or massie, that a man may be hurt mortally by one of them; but these commonly come from the *Mauquáuwogs*, [Mohawk Indians, Iroquois] or the *Men eaters*, three or four hundred miles from us: They have an excellent Art to cast our *Pewter* and *Brasse* into very neate and artificiall *Pipes*: They make their *Wuttammâuog* (that is, a weake *Tobacco*) which the men plant themselves, very frequently; yet I never see any take so excessively .... (Roger Williams, 1643)

The Calumet

When the French sailed into Narragansett Bay in 1556, they saw an Indian smoking a bowl with a long stem, and they called this the *calumet*.

So the peace pipe was first called the calumet here in Narragansett country.

The peace pipe has something from the stone and mineral kingdoms, the wood, plant, and animal kingdoms and some leather trimming. Everything that went for peace and maintenance went on to that pipe.

And when he smoked that pipe, and made a treaty with any of the settling of America, that smoke went to heaven and sealed his word with his Creator.

You will find nowhere in history where the Indian was the first to break his word, because his word was sealed with his Creator. (Princess Red Wing, 1986)

Origin of Drum [*popowuttáhig*]

Now, it's a beautiful day today, and I'm reminded of a young Indian who stood on a hilltop with all the glories of nature around him. He felt so good that his heart beat, and he heard 1-1-1-1.

And when he realized how close he was to Mother Nature, he settled upon the grass, and he fed from the berries on the bushes, and the fish from the sea, and he heard 1-2, 1-2, 1-2, 1-2.

And he realized everything his eyes beheld—the high trees, the green grass, the hills, the rocks, the rushing waters, and even himself—was created by a good and great and unseen spirit. He heard the heartbeat of the Creator of the universe. He heard 1-2-3, 1-2-3, 1-2-3, 1-2-3.

As soon as he recognized his Creator, he looked beside him and saw his brother. Then he heard the heartbeat of mankind and he heard 1-2-3-4, 1-2-3-4, 1-2-3-4, 1-2-3-4.

Then he made up his drum and beat out that rhythm. And all of his business meetings and all of his ceremonies are called together by the beat of the drum. And when the drum speaks people come, sit in a circle and are quiet until they are asked to speak. (Princess Red Wing, 1986)

[When] they winter, they remove a little neerer to their Summer fields; when 'tis warme Spring, then they remove to their fields where they plant Corne.

In middle of Summer, because of the abundance of Fleas, which the dust of the house breeds, they will flie and remove on a sudden from one part of their field to a fresh place: And sometimes having fields a mile or two, or many miles asunder, when the worke of one field is over, they remove house to the other: If death fall in amongst them, they presently remove to a fresh place: If an enemie approach, they remove into a Thicket, or Swampe, unless they have some Fort to remove unto.

Sometimes they remove to a hunting house in the end of the yeere, and forsake it not until Snow lie thick, and then will travel home, men, women and children, thorow the snow thirtie, yea fiftie or sixtie miles; but their great remove is from the Summer fields to warme and thicke woodie bottomes where they winter: They are quicke; in halfe a daye, yea, sometimes at few houres warning to be gone and the house up elsewhere; especially, if they have stakes readie pitch for their *Mats*.

I once in travell lodged at a house, at which in my returne I hoped to have lodged againe there the next night, but the house was gone in that interim, and I was glad to lodge under a tree.

The men make the poles or stakes, but the women make and set up, take downe, order, and carry the *Mats* and hous-holdstuffe. (Roger Williams, 1643)

[AUTHOR'S NOTE—European writers describe native women as being almost slave-like in their roles. Let's see what a 16-year old adopted white girl has to say. Dickewamis (her Indian name means something like "A Pretty Girl") was captured and adopted by the Seneca in 1755. She married and was just like all the other Indian women in the village. She said "Our labour was not severe.... Their task is probably not harder than white women who have these articles provided for them; and their cares certainly are not half as numerous, nor as great [as Whites]... we could work as we pleased." (J. E. Seaver (1824), *A Narrative of the Life of Mrs. Mary Jemison*, pp. 46-47)]

THE BODY & SENSES

Their Hardiness

Beat them, whip them, pinch them, punch them, if they resolve not to wince for it, they will not.... The unexpected approach of a mortal wound by a bullet, an arrow, or sword strikes no more terror, cause no more exclamation, no more complaint or winceing than if it had been shot into a tree... some of them having been shot in at the mouth and out under the ear, some shot in the breast, some run through and other many desperate wounds, which they either by their rare skill in the use of vegatatives or diabolical charms they are in short time... [cured]. (William Wood, 1634; quoted in Lenz, 1995b, p. 76)

Amazing Eyesight and Sense of Smell

I have observed that the Salvages have the sence of seeing so farre beyond any of our Nation, that one would allmost beleeve they had intelligence from the Devill, sometimes: when they have tould us of a shipp at Sea, which they have seene soener [sooner] by one hower [hour], yea two howers sayle, then any English man that stood by; of purpose to looke out, their sight is so excellent. This I am sure, I have well observed in the sense of smell, they have a great perfection: which is confirmed by the opinion of the French that are planted about Canada, who have made relation that they are so perfect in the use if that sense, that will distinguish between a Spaniard and a Frenchman by the sent [sense] of the hand only. (Thomas Morton,

1632; quoted in Lenz, 1995b, p. 52)

They were thereby accustomed at a young age to work, as well as to everything they had to do, even to [eating] the Fir gum [canoe sealant]. In consequence they never had toothache, and their teeth were well kept and white as snow. (Nicholas Denys quoted in Lenz, 1995c, p. 160.)

In the braine their opinion is, that the soule... keeps her chiefe seat and residence: For the temper of the braine in quick apprehensions and accurate judgements (to say no more) the most high and soveraign God and Creator, hath not made them inferior. (Roger Williams, 1643)

The Tooth-ake

... which is the only paine will force their stout hearts to cry; I cannot heare of any disease of the stone amongst them (the corne of the Countrey, with which they are fed from the wombe, being an admirable cleanser and opener) but the paine of their womens childbirth... never forces their women to cry, as I have heard some of their men in this paine.
    In this paine they use a certaine root dried, not much unlike our *Ginger*. (Roger Williams, 1643)

Sometimes a man shall meet a lame man or an old man with a Staffe: but generally a Staffe is a rare sight in the hand of the eldest, their Constitution is so strong. I have upon occasion travelled many a score, yea many a hundreth mile amongst them, without need of stick or staffe, for any appearance of danger amongst them; yet it is a rule amongst them, that it is not good for a man to travell without a Weapon nor alone. (Roger Williams, 1643)

DISCOURSE AND NEWS & ORAL HISTORY

Their manner is upon any tidings to sit around, double or treble, or more, as their numbers be I have seene neer a thousand in a round, where *English* could not well neere halfe so many have sitten: Every man hath his pipe of their *Tobacco*, and a deepe silence they make, and attention give to him that speaketh; and many of them will deliver themselves, either in a relation of news, or in a consultation, with very emphaticall speech and great action, commonly an houre, and sometimes two houres together. (Roger Williams, 1643)

Why Did the English Come Here?

The question they oft put to me: why come the *Englishmen* hither? and measuring others by ourselves; they say, It is because you want *firing:* [fire-wood] for they, having burnt up the *wood* in one place, (wanting draughts to bring *wood* to them) they are faine to follow the *wood*; and so to remove to a fresh new place for the *woods* sake. (Roger Williams, 1643)

Recording Oral History

... instead of records and chroncicles they take this course: Where any remarkable act is done, in memory of it, either in the place or by some pathway near adjoining, they make a round hole in the ground about a foot deep and as much over: which when others passing by, behold, they enquire the cause and occasion of the same; which being once known, they are careful to acquaint all men as ocassion serveth therewith.

And lest holes should be filled or grown up [with herbage] by any accident, as men pass by they will oft renew the same. By which means, many things of great antiquity are fresh in memory. So that as a man travelleth, if he can understand his guide, his journey will be less tedious by reason of the many historical discourses [that] will be related to him. (Edward Winslow, *Good News from New England*, 1624; quoted in Lenz, 1995b, p. 11)

Elder's History

My Fathers
My fathers were they who first met you
Where the tide of the great waters flow
Far, far to the east as the arrow flies
Ten thousand moons ago

My fathers who roamed through the forest
My fathers by river and sea
Who roamed through their vast dominions
Like the winds of the heavens as free

They were brothers to the storm and the sunshine
They were brothers to the oak and the pine
They were shadows that strolled with moccasin feet
Through the glade where the wild grapes twine
No fear of the lightning's terror
No fear of the wolves' hungry cry
While the smoke of their many wigwams sailed calmly against the sky

So lived my fathers O Pale Face
They were children of the vast and the wild
They were happy within their borders
In a land that was undefiled

Then one day from across the waters
A speck gloomed dark across the sky
And shadows ran swift through the forest
While the night owl hooted his cry

Then my fathers went down to your fathers
While the keel grated harsh against the sands
They welcomed your fathers O Pale Face
With a pipe of peace in their hands.

(Princess Red Wing, 1986)

They want to dry the tears that drowned
the sun
They want laughter to return to their hearts
They want to go home—to Mother and
Grandmother
They want to hear their ancestral voices
'round the fire.

(Moondancer, *Wampumpeag*, 1996)

TIME

The people are very ingenious and obervative. They keep account of time by the moon and [by] winters and summers. They know divers of the stars by name. In particular they know the North Star and call it *Maske*, which is to say "The Bear." (Edward Winslow, 1624; quoted in Lenz, 1995b, p. 11)

They are punctuall in measuring their *Day* by the *Sunne*, and their *Night* by the *Moon* and the *Starres*; and their lying abroad in the ayre, and so living in the open fields, occasioneth even the youngest amongst them to be very observent of those *Heavenly* Lights. (Roger Williams, 1643)

Without Clocks or Watches, They Tell Time After Their Own Fashion

And then they point with the hand to the Sunne, by whose highth they keepe account of the day, and by the Moone and Stars by night, as wee doe by clocks and dials &c. "I will come when the sun is thus high"—*Yo taunt nippeean*. (Roger Williams, 1643)

They are punctuall in their promises of keeping time; and sometimes have charged mee with a lye for not punctually keeping time, though hindered. (Roger Williams, 1643)

Time was marked on the time sticks and the ages of the children recorded. Time was figured so many harvest back or so many harvests in the future.... (Princess Red Wing, in Kaiser, p. 4)

SEASONS

They have thirteen *Moneths* according to the severall *Moones*; and they give each of them significant names.... (Roger Williams, 1643)

Rain Dance

If the yeere proove drie, they have great and solemne meetings from all parts at one high place, to supplicate their gods, and to beg raine, and they will continue in their worship ten dayes; a fortnight; yea, three weeks, until raine come. (Roger Williams, 1643)

Every moon was the ocassion of a Ceremony or Festival of Thanks. (Princess Red Wing, in Kaiser, p. 4)

According to the Indians there were 13 moons during the year, which extended from one harvest to the next, and the moons were counted by the 13 squares on the turtles' back. The turtle, is therefore, one of the special totems of many different tribes of Indians. (Princesss Red Wing, in Kaiser, p. 1)

Wampanoag/Narragansett Seasons

Fall   'ninnauwāet
Winter   poponăe
Spring   sequan
Summer   nepinnāe

(Strong Woman and Moondancer, *A Massachusett Language Book, Vol. 1*)

TRAVEL

I t is admirable to see, what paths their naked hardened feet have made in the wildernesse in most stony and rockie places. (Roger Williams, 1643)

They are joyfull in meeting any in travell, and will strike fire with stones or sticks, to take Tobacco, and discourse a little together. (Roger Williams, 1643)

Run 80-100 Miles in One Day

They are generally quick on foot, brought up from the breasts to running: Their legs being also from the wombe stretcht and bound up in a strange way on their Cradle backward, as also annointed; yet have they some that excell: so that I have knowne many of them run betweene fourescore or an hundred miles in a Summers day, and back within two dayes: they doe also practice running of *Races*; and commonly in the Summer, they delight to doe without shoes, although they have them hanging at their backs: they are so exquisitely skilled in all the body and bowels of the Countrey (by reason of their huntings) that I have often been guided twentie, thirtie, sometimes fortie miles through the woods, a streight course, out of any path. (Roger Williams, 1643)

Making Fires

A good well growne deere skin is of great account with them; and it must have the tale [tail] on, or else they account it defaced... [which] when they travell is raped [wrapped] round their body and, with a girdle of their making, bowl around their middles, to which girdle is fastened a bagg, in which his instruments be with which he can strike fire upon any occasion. (Thomas Morton, 1632; quoted in Lenz, 1995b, p. 44)

These thick Woods and Swamps... are the Refuges for Women and children in Warre, whil'st the men fight. As the Countrey is wondrous full of Brookes and Rivers, so doth it also abound with fresh ponds, some of many miles compasse. (Roger Williams, 1643)

If any Robbery fall out in Travell, between Persons of diverse States, the offended State sends for Justice; if no Justice bee granted and recompence made, they grant out a kind of letter of Mart to take satisfaction themselves, yet they are careful not to exceed in taking from others, beyond the Proportion of their owne losse. (Roger Williams, 1643)

I could never heare that Murthers or Robberies are comparably so frequent, as in parts of *Europe* among the English, French &c. [when traveling]. (Roger Williams, 1643)

The Indian Canoe—A Marvelous Invention

For their water passage, travels and fishing, they make boats, or canoes, either of great trees, pine or chestnut, made hollow, and artificially; which they do by burning them; and after with tools, scraping, smoothing, shaping. Of these they make greater or lesser [in size]. Some I have seen will carry twenty persons, being forty or fifty feet in length, as broad as the tree will bear.

    They make another sort of canoes of birchen bark, which they close together, sewing them with a kind of bark, and them smearing the places with turpentine of the pine tree. They are strengthened in the inside with some few timbers and ribs; yet they are so light, that one man will, and doth, ordinarily carry one of them upon his back several miles, that will transport five or six people.... (Gookin, 1674, pp. 12-13)

Origin of JOHNNY CAKE

If their imperious occasions cause them to travel, the best of their victuals for their journey is *nocake* (as they call it), which is nothing but Indian corn parched in the hot ashes.... With this strange viaticum they will travel [called JOURNEY CAKE, then JOHNNY CAKE] four or five days together, with loads fitter for elephants than men. (Wm. Wood, 1634; quoted in Lenz, 1995b, p. 72)

THE HEAVENS AND HEAVENLY BODIES

By which they acknowledge the Sun, and adore for a God or divine power. (Roger Williams, 1643)

By occasion of their frequent lying in the Fields and Woods, they much observe the Starres, and their very children can give Names to many of them, and observe their Motions, and they have the same words for their rising, courses, and setting, as for the Sun or Moone, as before.

Mosk or *Paukúnawaw* the great Beare... which words *Mosk*, or *Paukúnawaw* signifies a Beare, which is so much the more observable, because, in most Languages that signe or Constellation is called the Beare.

Shwishcuttowwáuog [is] The Golden Metewand [belt of Orion]. Mishánnock [is] the morning Starre. Chippápuock [is] the Brood Hen [Pleiades], &c. (Roger Williams, 1643)

More From Voyages of Italian Explorer Giovanni da Verrazzano
Newport, RI

... When sowing, they observe the influence of the moon, the rising of the Pliedes, and many other customs derived from the ancients. (quoted in Bragdon, 1996, p. 124)

Their food is pulse [peas, beans, etc.], as with other tribes, which is here better than elsewhere, and more carefully cultivated; in the time of sowing they are governed by the moon, the sprouting of grain, and many other ancient usages. (from *The Voyages of Giovanni da Verrazzano, 1524-1528;* quoted in Lenz, 1994, p. 31)

WEATHER

Also they have many names for the winds. They will guess at the wind and weather beforehand, by observations in the heavens. They report also that some of them can cause the wind to blow in what part they list [and] can raise storms and tempests. Which they do when they intend the death or destruction of other people.... (Edward Winslow, 1624; quoted in Lenz, 1995b, p. 11)

It may bee wondred why since *New-England* is about 12 degrees neerer to the Sun, yet some part of Winter it is there ordinarily more cold than here in *England*: the reason is plaine: All Ilands are warmer than maine Lands and Continents. *England* being an Iland, *Englands* winds are Sea winds, which are commonly more thick and vapoury, and warmer winds: The *Nor West* wind (occasioneth *New-England* cold) comes over the cold frozen Land, and over many millions of Loads of Snow: and yet the pure wholsomnesse of the Aire is wonderfull, and the warmth of the Sunne, such in the sharpest weather, that I have often seen the Natives Children runne about starke naked in the coldest dayes, and the *Indians*, Men and Women, lye by a Fire, in the Woods in the coldest nights, and I have been often out my selfe such nights without fire, mercifully, and wonderfully preserved. (Roger Williams, 1643)

kussútah = "it's hot today"   vs   *tohquoi* = "it is cold"

THE WINDS

Some of them account of seven, some eight, or nine; and in truth, they doe upon the matter reckon and observe not onely the foure but the eight Cardinall winds.... (Roger Williams, 1643)

[The southwest wind] is the pleasingest, warmest wind in the Climate, most desired of the *Indians*, making faire weather ordinarily; and therefore they have a *Tradition*, that to the Southwest, which they call *Sowwaníu*, the gods chiefly dwell; and hither the soules of all their Great and Good men and women goe.

The Southwest wind is called by the *New-English*, the Sea turne, which comes from the Sunne in the morning, about nine or ten of the clock Southeast, and about South, and then strongest Southwest in the after-noone, and towards night, when it dies away.

It is rightly called the Sea turne, because the wind commonly all the Summer, comes off from the North and Northwest in the night, and then turnes about from the South in the day.... (Roger Williams, 1643)

BIRDS

Blackbirds [chóganeuck]

Of this sort there be millions, which are great devourers of the *Indian* corne as soon as it appeares out of the ground .... (Roger Williams, 1643)

Crows [kaukontuock]

These Birds, although they doe the corne also some hurt, yet scarce will one *Native* amongst an hundred kil them, because they have a tradition, that the Crow brought them at first an *Indian* Graine of Corne in one Eare, and an *Indian* or *French* Beane in another, from the Great God *Kautántouwits* field in the Southwest, from whence they hold all their Corne and Beanes. (Roger Williams, 1643)

Ducks [quequécummaûog]

The *Indians* having abundance of these sorts of Foule upon the waters, take great pains to kill any of them with their Bow and Arrowes [using look-alike decoys and imitative sounds]; and are marvellous desirous of our *English* Guns, powder, and shot (though they are wisely and generally denied by the *English*) yet with those which they get from the *French*, and some others (*Dutch* and *English*) they kill abundance of Fowle, being naturally excellent marks-men; and also more hardened to endure the weather, and wading, lying, and creeping on the ground &c.

I once saw an exercise of training of the *English*, when all the *English* had mist the mark set up to shoot at, an *Indian* with his owne Peece (desiring leave to shoot) only hit it. (Roger Williams, 1643)

Pigeon-country [wuskowhanaûke]

In that place these *Fowle* breed abundantly, and by reason of their delicate Food (especially in Strawberrie time when they pick up whole large Fields of the old grounds of the *Natives*) they are a delicate fowle, and because of their abundance, and the facility of killing of them, they are and may be plentifully fed on.

Sachim: a little Bird about the bignesse of a swallow, or lesse, to which the *Indians* give that name, because of its *Sachim* or Princelike courage and Command over greater Birds, that a man shall often see this small Bird pursue and vanquish and put to flight the Crow, and other Birds fare bigger then it selfe. (Roger Williams, 1643)

How The Birds Got Their Songs

Now, Indian children didn't have toys and bicycles and tricycles and all kinds of toys like you have today. So they played with the things of nature. And one of the things they'd love to do in the Fall when the leaves turned and they'd drop to the ground was to make big piles of leaves and they'd roll in them. The dogs would roll in there with them, and they really had a lot of fun in those Autumn leaves.

Then the snow would come and cover the leaves and turn them brown and die. The Indian children would say to the Great Spirit, "Oh, we wish the leaves could live forever." So, the Great Spirit, to please his Indian children said, "I'll let some of the leaves live forever."

So out of the yellow ones he made the canaries. And they began to fly around and around and around. And out of the red ones he made the cardinals. And they began to fly around and around and around. Out of the speckled ones he made the orioles, and out of the brown ones he made the sparrow and the thrush.

Well, the Indian children became so happy, they had the birds flying all around them. But the birds were very unhappy because they did not have their song.

So the wise old owl called a council. The birds all came in and sat in a circle. And then the old owl told them, "To get your song you must fly to heaven to get it."

Now you know, when you start to do something there's always someone who wants to be first, never wants to get in line and take his place. Well, that was the old crow. He said, "Me first, me first." So he went up a little way, and came back down with a "caw, caw, caw."

Then there's always someone who calls out, "Me next," and never wants to wait their turn. That was the old blue jay. So the blue jay says, "Me next, me next." He went up and came back with a "chirp, chirp, chirp."

But some of the birds were very polite and waited their turn to go up one-by-one to get their song. And the little meadowlark who waited her turn came back with a beautiful song because she waited her turn.

Then the little woodland thrush said, "I wish I could have a song that sweet, but I don't think I can fly that high." So she sat right next to the great eagle, and climbed right on the back of his neck and cuddled down right among his neck feathers. And when that great bird started up and up and up on his great wings, there was the little woodland thrush. When he went up as far as his wings would take him, he started back down. She flew off, and she went further up and up and up until she received the sweetest song from heaven. But she was so far up, that it took her so long to get back down.

And when she got back down, all the birds had been up, and all had their songs, and they looked at her and she looked at them. She was so ashamed because they knew she had cheated. And she walked right out of that circle way back into the woods. And to this day she has never come out.

So, if you want to hear the woodland thrush sing, you have to be way back in the woods. You have to be very, very quiet and you will hear the sweetest song from heaven. (Princess Red Wing, 1986)

THE EARTH & PLANTING CROPS

Slash and Burn to Keep Country Fertile

The savages are accustomed to set fire to the Country in all places... twize a year; viz, at the spring, and the fall.... The reason that mouves them to doe so is because it would otherwise be so overgrown with underweeds... and the people would not be able in any wise to passe through the Country out of a beaten path. The means they they do it with is with a certain mineral stone, that they carry about them in baggs... carrying in the same a peece of touch wood... of their own making. (Thomas Morton, 1632, quoted in Lenz, 1995b, p. 54)

The *Natives* are very exact and punctuall in the bounds of their Lands, belonging to this or that Prince or People (even to a River, Brooke &c). And I have knowne them make bargaine and sale amongst themselves for a small piece, or quantity of Ground.... (Roger Williams, 1643)

There be diverse sorts of this Corne, and of the colours: yet all of it either boild in milke, or buttered. If the use of it were knowne and received in *England* (it is the opinion of some skilled in physick) it might save many thousand lives in *England,* occasioned by the binding nature of *English* wheat, the *Indian* Corne keeping the body in a constant moderate loosenesse. (Roger Williams, 1643)

The Women set or plant, weede, and hill, and gather and barne all the corne, and Fruites of the field: Yet sometimes the man himselfe, (either out of love to his wife, or care for his Children, or being an old man) will help the Woman which (by the custome of the Countrey) they are not bound to.

When a field is to be broken up, they have a very loving sociable speedy way to dispatch it: All the neighbors men and Women forty, fifty, a hundred &c, joyne, and come in to help freely.

With friendly joyning they break up their fields, build their Forts, hunt the Woods, stop and kill fish in the Rivers.... (Roger Williams, 1643)

Asqútasquash, their Vine aples, which the *English* from them call *Squashes* about the bignesse of Apples of severall colours, a sweet, light wholesome refreshing. (Roger Williams, 1643)

In the month of May was held this festival [Festival of Planting] during the Moon of Planting. The dances and chants used for the ceremony were very dramatic, especially the Corn Dance. The movements illustrated the planting of the seed and patting the earth into the prayers for rain. At this time of the year the Indians moved to the open country along the Bay where they could plant their crops. (Princess Red Wing, in Kaiser, p. 9)

Story of Succotash

Our State name, Rhode Island and Providence Plantations, tells us that these fertile grounds were once the great garden of my ancestors. Everything his eyes beheld—the fruits and nut trees, edible roots, stems, and flowers, wild berries of every kind, and all the bounty in between, was created by the Great Spirit for his children, the Indian people. The Indian called this place *Ohke* (ahkee), Mother Earth, because she provided him with all his needs.

As far as I can remember, some of the early cooked foods of the Indians were parched corn, broiled fish, roasted game, boiled corn meal, stewed beans, and succotash. These foods, according to our oral traditions, were created by the Great Spirit many moons ago for the maintenance of mankind.

It is also believed that the corn (*weatchimmineash*) and the beans (*manusqussedash*) were brought by the crow (or *kaukont*), and therefore were cooked in a pot together. We called this nourishing dish, *m'sickquatash* (succotash).

Since the crow brought the new food, he was a sacred bird. He was never harmed and became a respected tribal totem. The Indians caught, tamed and trained hawks to chase the crows from the cornfields. Young boys were also given the task of sitting in the fields upon a high, wooden platform to ward off the crows. And when the young boys became weary of chasing the crows, they would hang their mantels (jacket) on a stick from the platform and run off to play. This practice became the basis for our modern-day scarecrow seen in every garden and farm all across America today.

Now, let me tell you a story that all Indian children are told by their grandmothers. It is thousands of years old.

> When the Indian man hunted ages ago, they hunted for the whole village, leaving small children, women and the old ones at home. Sometimes the hunters were gone for so long that the people in the village became very hungry. So the old medicine man sent up a prayer to the Great Spirit asking for food for the people of his village. The Great Spirit heard the cries and summoned the crow to fly to his Great Garden in the Southwest. There the Great Spirit placed a kernel of corn in one ear and a bean in the other and told the crow to fly back to his children in the East. The crow, with the corn and the bean, flew over the village and threw down the precious seeds. Just then, the crow was given momentarily a human voice and he uttered "succotash" (which means to mix). Then his tongue was sealed and he never spoke again. Since that time, people have heard the crow chant his song of a job well done— 'caw, caw, caw'.
>
> As instructed, the Indian then planted these seeds together along with squash in a single mound of rich, black earth using dead fish as fertilizer. When harvested in the fall, it gave the Indian people a valuable food source. They cooked it up together and succotash became a favorite dish among the Narragansett, Wampanoag, Mohegan and other woodland tribes.

We have a song and a dance that honors the crow for his contribution to the survival of the Woodland Indians. Well, that's the story I learned. Now let me fill in some details about these precious foods.

The Three Sisters

Corn supplied the eastern woodland tribes with a valuable food source. It produced starch to make energy, and provided the body with seventy-five percent of its daily needs for survival. Beans (as a protein source) and squash (vitamin c) were planted in the same fields. The corn stalk and its roots kept everything well anchored. The bean twined around the corn stalk for support and the squash choked out the weeds and also kept the root system well hydrated. The Indians believed that these foods had spirit beings and called these foods the "three sisters" because they supported each other as they grew just like sisters do. Dried and stored, corn, bean and squash guaranteed the Indian good eating all year long.

Seasons

According to tradition, there were 13 full moons during the year, which extended from one harvest to the next. The moons were counted by the thirteen large squares on the turtles' back. The smaller squares found on the outer edge of the shell were notched off to keep track of the days. It takes 28 days before a new moon appears. If you multiply 13 by 28 this equals 364!

Although there are 365 days in a calendar year, this was a pretty accurate time piece that aided the Indian to plant or harvest his garden (*tanohketeaonk*). Another method was to observe the size of the tree buds. When the buds became as large as a squirrels ear, usually around the month of May, it was time to plant the corn. We also know that Indians throughout the Americas were expert astronomers, and used knowledge of the heavens [such as Pleides constelation] to guide them in things like planting seasons. Among my people this knowledge was not recorded.

We had special names for our calendar just as today we have Christmas in December, day light saving time, etc.

The names of our months are based on the moons. [Please note: Our new calendar year starts in May. This is based on our planting practices.]

The Moons

New Year Moon or Planting Moon (Mid/late May)	Aukeeteaumitch Nepaúzshad
Strawberry Moon (June)	Wuttahminneoh Nepaúzshad
Burning Moon (July)	Chikotae Nepaúzshad
Greenbean Moon (August)	Ashashki Tuppuhquam Nepaúzshad
Ripe Corn Moon (September)	Kesanoohteau Nepaúzshad
Harvest Moon (October)	Kepenum Nepaúzshad
Hunting Moon (November)	Adchaeu Nepaúzshad
Giving Moon (December)	Maguntche Nepaúzshad
Freezing Moon (January)	Taquattin Nepaúzshad
First Thaw Moon (February)	Negonne Michokat Nepaúzshad
Sugaring Moon (March)	Wekonash Nepaúzshad
Melting Moon (April)	Adbohteau Nepaúzshad
Fishing Moon (Early May)	Kuttaumen Nepaúzshad

(Strong Woman, 1999)

HELPING THE ENGLISH

Fish Fertilizer for Good Indian Corn

Afterwards they, as many as were able, began to plant their corn. In which service Squanto stood them in great stead; showing them, both the manner how to set it and after how to dress and tend it. And he told them..., [to get] fish and set with it [ie, manure the ground with alewives at the time of setting]; in these old grounds, it would come to nothing. And he showed them that in the middle of April they should have store enough [of fish] come[ing] up the brook by which they began to build, and taught them how to take it. And where to get other provisions necessary for them. All which they found true by trial and experience.... (*Mourt's Relation*, 1622; quoted in Lenz, 1995a, p. 42)

Other Ways Our Ancestors Helped the English

[In] many ways hath their advice and endeavor been advantageous unto us, they being our first instructors for the planting of their Indian corn, by teaching us to cull out the finest seed, to observe the fittest season, to keep distance for holes and fit measure for hills, to worm and weed it, to prune it, and dress it as occasion shall require.... These Indians are very hospitable, insomuch as when the English have traveled forty, fifty, or threescore miles into the country, they have entertained them into their houses, quartered them by themselves in the best rooms, providing their best victuals they could.... Many other wandering, benighted coasters have been kindly entertained into their habitations, where they have rested and reposed themselves more securely than if they had been in some blind obscure England's inn.... Many lazy boys that have run-away from their masters have been brought home by these ranging foresters.... (Wm. Wood, 1634; quoted in Lenz, 1995b, pp. 73-74)

FIRST THANKSGIVING DAY

English Story

You shall understand that in this little time [Dec. 16, 1621] that a few of us have been here, we have built seven dwelling houses; and four for the use of the Plantation: and have made preparation for divers others.

We set, last Spring, some twenty acres of Indian corn; and sowed some six acres of barley and pease [peas]: and according to the manner of the Indians, we manured our ground with herrings, or rather shads [alewives]; which we have in good abundance, and take with great ease at our doors [in the Town Brook].

Our corn did prove well, and GOD be praised! We had a good increase of Indian corn; and our barley indifferent good; but our pease not worth the gathering; for we feared they were too late sown. They came up very well, and blossomed: but the sun parched them in the blossom.

Our Harvest being gotten in, our Governour [Wm Bradford] sent four men on fowling; that so we might, after a more special manner, rejoice together, after we had gathered the fruit of our labours [in what would become known popularly as the first (Anglo-American) Thanksgiving Day]. They four, in one day, killed as much fowl [and the plentiful turkeys] as, with a little help besides, served the Company [about 50 people by then] almost a week. At which time amongst other recreations, we exercised our Arms many of the Indians coming amongst us.

And amongst the rest, their greatest King, Massasoyt, with some ninety men; whom for three days, we entertained and feasted.

And they [the Wampanoag] went out and killed five deer: which they brought to the Plantation; and bestowed on our Governour, and upon the Captain [Miles Standish], and others. (Edward Winslow, Dec., 1621; quoted in Lenz, 1995a, p. 56).

The Wampanoag Story

Now when the Pilgrims came over, they had a hard time and might have all starved if the Wampanoag Indians from the other side of the bay in Massachusetts had not opened up their storehouses and fed them and showed them how to fertilize the virgin soil with dead fish.

When another cold winter was ahead of them, and since many had died and their crops had been poor, the Pilgrims didn't feel very festive.

However, old Squanto went to Plimouth Plantation and said to Governor Bradford, "When things look dark and your crops are poor, and many pass into the land of the Hereafter, then *this* is the time for the biggest feast and the longest dance to give thanks to your Creator and show Him you are not complaining against your hard lot."

Governor Bradford answered and said, "That would be good for my fainting people. Go! Call your Massasoit and your people and tell them to come, and we will have feast and thank God for the blessings we have."

The Indians came with their wild turkey, deer and bear meat, potatoes, corn, beans, squash, pumpkins, melons and cranberries. There was enough to feed all Plimouth and themselves, and they cooked it, sat down, ate and thanked God.

History says that was the first Thanksgiving in America, and it *was*... for *them*, those Pilgrims. However, to *my ancestors*, it was just *another* Thanksgiving, for the harvest of the garden, the forest, the fields, and the meadows....

We celebrated four *other* Thanksgivings! Ceremonies were held throughout the year for our people where we could give thanks for our blessings.... (Princess Red Wing, 1986)

ANIMALS

More From the Voyages of Italian Explorer Giovanni da Verrazzano, Newport, RI

The animals, which are in great numbers, as stags, deer, lynxes, and many other species, are taken by snares, and by bows, the latter being their cheif implement; their bows are wrought with great beauty, and for the heads of them, they use emery, jasper, hard marble, and other sharp stones, in the place of iron. (from *The Voyages of Giovanni da Verrazzano, 1524-1528;* quoted in Lenz, 1994, p. 31)

The Conie (Rabbit, Hare) [môhtukquás]

They have a reverend esteeme of this Creature, and conceive there is some Deity in it. (Roger Williams, 1643)

Black Foxes

The *Indians* say they have black Foxes, which they have often seene, but never could take any of them: they say they are *Manittóoes*, that is, Gods, Spirits or Divine powers.... (Roger Williams, 1643)

The Rabbit Story

A little rabbit went out to walk on a cool day in the Fall. Oh, it was real cool.

And he came to a willow tree, and so he began to dance around and around. Well, by and by the wind came up and he began to shiver. "Oh, it's kinda cool."

So he danced faster and faster around the willow tree. After awhile he looked up into the sky. And he said, "I think it's going to snow."

By and by it did snow. So he danced faster and faster around the willow tree and patted the snow all down.

By and by he became so tired that he sat down on a limb of the willow tree and went to sleep.

He slept so long that when he awoke all the snow had melted and down below was all green.

Now you know the rabbit is a very timid animal. He was sitting up in the willow tree and he was afraid to jump out of a tree.

He was very hungry. He shut his eyes up tight and fell right out of that tree.

When he did, he cut his upper lip on a sharp stone. Now every rabbit has a split upper lip.

But when he fell out of that tree, he jammed his front legs right up into his body. Now every single rabbit and every single Easter Bunny has two short legs.

But when he fell out of that tree, he caught his tail and now every single rabbit has a short tail.

Now, when you're driving through the country in the Spring next year, and you come to a willow tree and think you're picking pussy willows.... why all the little Indian children know that's where the rabbit left his tail on the willow tree. (Traditional; recorded in Princess Red Wing, 1986)

Massachusett Language: The Rabbit Story (Translated)

Unnehtongquat Papaume Môhtukquasms

Pasuk ksuk adt 'ninnauwet môhtukquasms quequéshau. Hó

m?cheke tohkoi.

    Pyau yean anumwussukuppe. Pumukau mehtugq waéenu kah waéenu. Teanuk waban ?tshoh. Sonkquesu. Wussin, "nussonkques".

    Popomshau mehtuhq nano. Náim ushpuhquaeu kesukquieu. Wussin, "Pish muhp?."

    Náim muhp?ï. Pumukau m?cheke waéenu kah waéenu anumwussukuppe. Togkodtam muhp? manunne.

    Náim saunum onk tohk?taau mehtugq yeuyeu onk kussukkoueu. Koueu nôadtuk. T?kshau. Muhp? mohtupohteau. Quinnupohke ashkashki.

    Noh wahteunk môhtukquasog, wahheau nag na sohqutteahauháog. Nagum nont qushitteaonk. Mat queshau wutche mehtukq. Paskánontam. Yânunum wuskesukquash onk queshau wutche mehtukq.

    Tiadche petshau kenompskut. Wussisset?n kuhkukque musquheongane. Yeuyeu nishnoh môhtukquas mahche pohki kuhkukque mussisst?n — mahche neese kuhkukque mussisst?nash.

    Asuh ahquompak kepshont wusseettash waapém?ash adt wuhhog. Yeuyeu nishnoh môhtukquas onk nishnoh "Easter Bunny" mahche neese tiohquekekontash.

    Aôóg adt touohkmuk onk nôk wompiyeuash dtannetuog ut anumwussukuppe nummukkiog Indiansog newutche môhtugquasmesog wussukqunnash.

Kesteausu

(Translated by authors)

How The Bear Lost His Tail

    The bear, of course, hibernates in the winter, but late one day this bear got hungry, so he came out of hibernation and went looking for something to eat.

    Well, on his way he met Mr. Fox. The fox had a nice string of fish, so he said to Mr. Fox, "Won't you give me one, I'm hungry; I haven't had anything to eat all winter." The fox said, "Oh go fish for yourself!" The bear said, "I don't know how to fish." Well, the fox said, "If you go out on the ice there, you'll find a hole where I got mine. Sit down over that hole and put your tail down in it. When you feel a tingle you know you got a fish, but if you want as many as I got, you have to sit there until you feel a tingle all the way around your tail."

So the bear went out and hunted around on the ice. And he found the hole that Mr. Fox had talked about, and sat down over it and put his tail down into it.

Well, he sat there and he sat there. Oh, it was a cold day in late Winter-early Spring. Well, by and by, he felt a tingle. Oh, he was so happy! Well, he says, "I'm gonna sit here until I have a whole string of fish like Mr. Fox had."

Well he sat there and he felt a tingle here and a tingle there, and a tingle all the way around his tail. "I guess I'll pull my tail in now." Well it was a cold day, and his tail had frozen. So he pulled and he pulled and he pulled. He couldn't get his tail out. By and by he gave a yank and yanked his tail right off!

Now every single bear has a short tail.

(Traditional; recorded in Princess Red Wing, 1986)

THE SEA

I have seene a Native goe into the woods with his hatchet, carrying only a Basket of Corn with him, & stones to strike fire when he had feld his tree (being a *chesnut*) he made him a little House or shed of the bark of it, he puts fire and followes the burning of it with fire, in the midst on many places: his corne he boyles and hath the Brook by him, and sometimes he angles for a little fish: but so hee continues burning and hewing untill he hath within ten or twelve dayes (lying there at his worke alone) finished, and (getting hands,) launched his Boate; with which afterward hee ventures out to fish in the Ocean. (Roger Williams, 1643)

It is wonderfull to see how they will venture in those Canoes, and how (being oft overset as I have my selfe been with them) they will swim a mile, yea two or more safe to Land: I having been necessitated to passe waters diverse times with them, it hath pleased God to make them many times the instruments of my preservation; and when sometimes in great danger I have questioned safety, they have said to me: Feare not, if we overset I will carry you safe to Land. (Roger Williams, 1643)

I have knowne thirty or forty of their Canowes fill'd with men, and neere more of their enemies in a Sea-fight. (Roger Williams, 1643)

How They Swim

For their swimming, it is almost natural, but much perfected by continual practice. Their swimming is... like [that of a] dog their arms before them cutting through the liquids with their right shoulder. In this manner they swim very swift and far, wither in rough or smooth waters, sometime for their ease lying as still as a log. Sometimes they will play the dive-doppers [underwater swimming] and come up in unexpected places. Their children likewise be taught to swim when they are very young. (Wm. Wood, 1634; quoted in Lenz, 1995b, pp. 82-83)

FISHING

Sturgeon [képosh]

The Natives venture one or two in a Canow, and with an harping Iron, or such like Instruments sticke this fish, and so hale it into their Canow; sometimes they take them by their nets, which they make strong of hemp. (Roger Williams, 1643) [AUTHOR'S NOTE: these shark-like fish could be very large. Its back was so hard [*képosh* = "impenetrable back"] that the Native Peoples learned to trick it into surfacing on its belly by going out at night with torch lights attached to their canoes.]

Their Nets [wutashabpoouh]

Which they will set thwart some little River or Cove wherein they kil Basse (at the fall of the water) with their arrows, or sharp sticks, especially if headed with Iron, gotten from the *English*. (Roger Williams, 1643)

Quahog [poquaûhock]

This the English call Hens, a little thick shel fish which the Indians wade deepe and dive for, and after they have eaten the meat there (in those which are good) they breake out of the shell, about half an inch of a blacke part of it, of which they make their *Suckaûhock*, or black money, which is to them pretious. (Roger Williams, 1643)

Periwinckle [meteaûhock]

Of which they make their *Wómpam*, or white money, of halfe the value of their *Suckaúhock*, or black money.... (Roger Williams, 1643)

The Natives take exceeding great pains in their fishing, especially in watching their seasons by night; so that frequently they lay their naked bodies many a cold night on the cold shoare about a fire of two or three sticks, and oft in the night search their Nets; and sometimes goe in and stay longer in frozen water. (Roger Williams, 1643)

CLOTHING

T hey have no *clothes*, *Books*, nor *Letters* , and conceive their *Fathers* never had.... (Roger Williams, *Introduction*, 1643)

They have a two-fold nakednesse: First ordinary and constant, when although they have a Beasts skin, or an English mantle on, yet that covers ordinarily but their hinder parts and all the foreparts from top to toe, (except their secret parts, covered with a little Apron...). I say all else open and naked.

    Their male children goe starke naked, and have no Apron untill they come to ten or twelve yeeres of age; their Female they, in a modest blush cover with a little Apron of an hand breadth from their very birth.

    Their second nakedness is when their men often abroad, and both men and women within doores, leave off their beasts skin, or English cloth, and so (excepting their little Apron) are wholly naked; yet but few of the women but will keepe their skin or cloth (though loose) neare to them ready to gather it up about them.

    Custome hath used their minds and bodies to it, and in such a freedom from any wantonnesse amongst them, as, (with griefe) I have heard of in *Europe*. (Roger Williams, 1643)

As their apparel they wear breeches [leggings] and stockings in one, like some Irish; which is made of deer skins and have shoes [mocassins] of the same leather. They also wear a deer skin loose about them like a cloak which they will turn to the weather [wind] side.... The men wear also, when they go abroad in cold weather, an otter or fox skin on their right arm; but only their bracer [wrist-guard] on the left.

Women and all of that sex wear stings [of beads] about their legs which the men never do. (Edward Winslow, 1624; quoted in Lenz, 1996b, p. 11)

Dying Clothes

Also here lies divers roots and berries wherewith the Indians dye excellent holding colours that no raine nor washing can alter. (Francis Higginson, 1630; quoted in Lenz, 1996b, p. 28)

In the wintertime the more aged of them wear leather drawers, in form like the Irish trousers.... Many of them wear skins about them, these some be bears' skins, moose skins, and beaver skins sewed together, otter skins, and raccoon skins, most of them in winter having his deep-furred cat skin like a long large muff, which he shifts to that arm which lieth most exposed to the wind. Thus clad, he bustles better through a world of cold in a frost-paved wilderness than the furred [European] citizens in his warmer stove. (William Wood, 1634, quoted in Lenz, 1995b, pp. 68-69).

Both these, shoes and stockins they make of their deere skin worne out, which yet being eccellently tann'd by them, is excellent for to travell in wet and snow; for it is so well tempered with oyle, that the water cleane wring out; and being hang'd up in the chimney, they presently drie without hurt, as my selfe hath often proved. (Roger Williams, 1643)

They also commonly paint these *Moose* and deere-skins for their Summer wearing, with varietie of formes and colours. (Roger Williams, 1643)

Their Tobacco-bag [petowwassinug]

...which hangs at their neck, or sticks at their girdle, which is to them in stead of an English pocket. (Roger Williams, 1643)

Tattooes

Many of the better sort bearing upon their cheeks certain portraitures of beasts, as bears, deer, moose, wolves, etc.; some of fowls, as of eagles, hawks, etc., which not a superficial painting but a certain incision, or else a raising of their skin by a small sharp instrument under which they convey a certain kind of black unchangeable ink which makes the desired form apparent and permanent. (William Wood, 1634, quoted in Lenz, 1995b, p. 69)

Our English clothes are so strange unto them, and their bodies inured so to indure the weather, that when (upon gift &c.) some of them have had *English* cloathes, yet in a showre of raine, I have seen them rather expose their skins to the wet then their cloaths, and therefore pull them off, and keep them drie. (Roger Williams, 1643)

Boys and girls may not wear their hair like men and women, but are distinguished thereby. (Winslow, 1624; quoted in Simmons, 1986, p. 47)

RELIGION

Where Do We Come From, And How Long Have We Been Here?

They say themselves, that they have *sprung* and *growne* up in that very place [homeland], like the *trees* of the *Wildernesse*. (Roger Williams, *Introduction*, 1643)

Creation Tale

At first, they say, there was no sachim, but Kiehtan, who dwelleth above in the heavens.... Never man saw this Kiehtan; only old men tell of him, and bid tell their children, yea to charge them to teach their posterities the same, and lay the like charge upon them.... (Winslow, 1624; quoted in Bragdon, p. 194)

Their religion is as other gentiles are. Some for their God adore the sun; others the moon; some the earth; others, the fire; and like vanities. Yet generally they acknowledge one great supreme being doer of good; and him they call Woonand, or Mannit: another that is the great doer of evil or mischief; and they call Mattand, which is their devil; and him they dread and fear, more than they love and honour the former good which is God. (Gookin, 1674, p. 14)

Kiehtan

Kiehtan... the principal and maker of all the rest [of the gods] and to be made by none... who dwelleth above in the heavens... for westward, wither all good men [and women] go when they die. (Winslow, 1624; quoted in Trumbull, 1903)

He that questions whether God made the World, the *Indians* will teach him. I must acknowledge I have received in my converse with them many Confirmation of these two great points:
1. That God is.
2. That hee is a rewarder of all them that diligently seek him.

They will generally confesse that God made all: but then in speciall, although they deny not that *English-mans* God made *English* Men, and the Heavens and earth there! yet their Gods made them, and the Heaven and Earth where they dwell. (Roger Williams, 1643)

They [Narragansetts] have many strange Relations of one *Wétucks*, a man that wrought many *Miracles* amongst them, and *walking upon the waters*, &c with some kind of broken Resemblance to the *Sonne* of God. (Roger Williams, *Inroduction*, 1643)

I have heard a poore *Indian* lamenting the losse of a child at break of day, call up his Wife and children, and all about him to Lamentation, with abundance of teares cry out! O God thou hast taken away my child! Thou art angry with me: O turne thine anger away from me, and spare the rest of my children.

If they received any good in hunting, fishing, Harvest &c. they acknowledge God in it.

Yea, if it be but an ordinary accident, a fall, &c. they will say God was angry and did it. *musquàntum manit*. God is angry....

First they branch their God-head into many Gods. Secondly, they attribute it to Creatures.

First, many Gods: they have given me the Names of thirty seven, which I have, all which in their solemne Worships they invocate: as *Kautántowwit* the great *South-West*, to whose House all souls goe, and from whom came the Corne, Beanes, as they say. (Roger Williams, 1643)

They Have More Than 38 Gods!

I find what I could never hear before, that they have plenty of Gods or divine powers: the Sunne, Moone, Water, Snow, Earth, the Deere, the Beare etc. are divine powers. I brought home lately from the Nanhiggonsicks [Narragansetts] the names of 38 of their Gods [most names seem to be lost] all that they could remember.... (Roger Williams, quoted in Bragdon, 1996, p. 186)

Missionaries on Martha's Vineyard

When the Lord first brought me to these poor Indians on the *Vinyard* they were mighty zealous and earnest in the Worship of false gods and Devils; their false gods were many, both of things in Heaven, Earth and Sea: And there they had their Men-gods, Women-gods, and Children-gods, their Companies, and Fellowships of gods, or Divine Powers, guiding things amongst men, innumerable more feigned gods belonging to many Creatures, to their Corn and every Colour of it: The Devil also with his Angels had his Kingdom among them, in them; account him they did the terror of Living, the god of the Dead, under whose cruel power and into whose deformed likeness they conceived themselves to be translated when they died; for the same word they have for *Devil,* they use for *a Dead Man,* in their Language. (John Eliot & Thomas Mayhew, 1653, pp. 201-202)

Fire God

When I argued with them about their Fire-God [Yotáanit]: can it, say they, be but this fire must be a God, or Divine power, that out of a stone will arise in a Sparke, and when a poore naked *Indian* is ready to starve with cold in the House, and especially in the Woods, often saves his life, doth dresse all our Food for us, and if he be angry will burne the House about us, yea if a spark fall into the drie wood, burnes up the Country? (though this burning of the Wood to them they count a Benefit, both for destroying of vermin, and keeping down the Weeds and thickets). (Roger Williams, 1643)

The Spirit of Hobomock [Abbomocho]

[Abbomocho] appeareth most ordinary and is most conversant with three sorts of people. One I confess I neither know by name nor office directly; of these they have few, but esteem highly of them, and think no weapon can kill them; another they call by the name powah, and the third pniese. (from Winslow; quoted in Bragdon, 1996, p. 214)

Hobomock or Abbomocho—Spirit of Death, Night, Northeast Wind, the Dark, Color Black, and Underworld

For their enemies and loose divers, whom they account unworthy of [paradise], they say that they pass to the infernal dwellings of Abamacho [*Abbomocho*], to be tortured according to the fictions of the ancient heathen. (from Wm. Wood, 1634; quoted in Bragdon, 1996, p. 189)

Hobomock or Abbomocho

Him they call upon to cure their wounds and diseases. When they are curable, he persuades them he sends the same for some conceived anger against them; but their calling upon him, can and doth help them; but when they are mortal and not curable in nature, then he persuades them Kiehtan is angry, and sends them, whom none can cure; insomauch as in that respect only they somewhat doubt whether be he simply good, and therefore in sickness never call upon him. (from Winslow, quoted in Bragdon, 1996, p. 189)

The Dream Soul of the Good and Great Goes to the Southwest, House of Great Spirit

...they hold the immortality of the never-dying soul that it shall pass to the southwest... holding it to be a kind of paradise wherein they shall everlastingly abide, solacing themselves in odoriferous gardens, fruitful corn fields, green meadows, bathing their tawny hides in the cool streams of pleasant rivers, and shelter themselves from heat and cold in the sumptuous palaces framed by the skill of natures curious contrivement. (from W. Wood, 1634; quoted in Bragdon, 1996, p. 191)

The Evil

Thither bad men go also, and knock at [Kiehtan's] door, but he bids them *quatchet*, that is to say, "Walk abroad!, for there is no place for such." So that they wander in restless want and penury. (from Winslow, 1624; quoted in Lenz, 199b, p. 6)

Spiritual Leaders

There are among them certain men and women, whom they call powows... partly are physicians, and make use... of herbs and roots, for curing the sick and diseased. (from Gookin; quoted in Bragdon, 1996, p. 201)

Powwáw ~ A Priest ["Medicine Man", Spiritual Leader]
Powwaûog ~ Priests

These doe begin and order their service, and Invocation of their Gods, and all he people follow, and joyne interchanageably in a laborious service, unto sweating, especially of the Priest, who spends himselfe in strange Antick Gestures, and Actions even unto fainting.
  In sickness the Priest comes close to the sick person, and performes many strange Actions about him, and threaten and conjures out the sickness. They conceive that there are many Gods or divine Powers within the body of a man: In his pulse, his heart, his Lungs, &c. (Roger Williams, 1643)

Spiritual Leaders

Their powows are reputed and I conceive justly, to hold familiarity with the devil; and therefore are by English laws, prohibited the exercise of their diabolical practices within the English jurisdiction, under the penalty of five pounds [or death]. (Gookin, 1674, p. 14)

Spiritual Leaders

The powah is eager and free in speech, fierce in countenance, and joineth many antic and laborious gestures with the same, over the partly diseased. If the party be wounded, he will also seem to suck the wound. (from Winslow; quoted in Bragdon, 1996, p. 204)

If the party be wounded, he will also seem to suck out the wound but if they be curable, as they say, he toucheth it not; but a *Skooke*, that is the snake, or *Wobsacuck*, that the eagle, sitteth on his shoulder, and licks the same. This none sees but the Powah who tells them, he doth it himself. (Winslow, 1624; quoted in Lenz, 1995b, p. 7)

[H]e wrapped a piece of cloth about the foot of the lame man [and] upon the wrapping of a beaver skin through which he—laying his mouth to the beaver skin—by his sucking charms he brought out the stump which he spat into a tray of water. (from Wm. Wood, 1634; quoted in Bragdon, 1996, p. 206)

Passaconaway
Famous Pawtucket *Nation Shaman & Powwaw (Spiritual Leader)*

...would goe under water to the further side of the river too broade for any man to undertake with a breath & deluding the company with casting a mist before their eies that see him enter in and come out... likewise by our English in the heat of summer to make Ice appeare in a bowl of faire water. (from Morton, 1632; quoted in Bragdon, 1996, p. 207)

More on Shaman Passaconaway

If we believe the Indians who report... he [*Passaconaway*] can make the water burn, the rocks move, the trees dance, metamorphise himself into a flaming man.... In the winter, when there is no green leaves to be got, he will burn an old one to ashes, and putting those into the water, produce a new green leaf... and make of a dead snakes' skin a living snake. (William Wood; quoted in Lenz, 1995b, p. 46)

Besides there is a general custome amongst them, at the apprehension of any Excellency in Men, Women, Birds, Beast, Fish, &c to cry out *Manittóo*, that is, it is a God, as thus if they see one man excell others in Wisdome, valour, strength, Activity &c they cry out *Manittóo* A God: and therefore when they talk amongst themselves of the *English* ships, and great buildings, of the plowing of their Fields, and especially of Bookes and Letters, they will end thus: *Manittôwock*. They are Gods: *Cummanittôo*, you are a God, &c. A strong conviction naturall in the soule of man, that God is; filling all things, and places, and that all Excellencies dwell in God, and proceed from him.... (Roger Williams, 1643)

Nickómmo ~ A Feast or Dance (Narragansett & Wampanoag)

Of this Feast they have publike, and private, and that of two sorts. First in sickness, or Drouth, or warre, or Famine. Secondly, After Harvest, after hunting, when they enjoy a caulme of peace, Health, Plenty, Prosperity, then *Nickómmo* a Feast, especially in Winter.... (Roger Williams, 1643)

He or she that make this *Nickómmo* Feast or Dance, besides the Feasting of sometimes twenty, fifty, an hundreth, yea I have seene neere a thousand persons at one of these Feasts, they give away I say a great quantity of money, and all sort of their goods (according to and sometimes beyond their estate) in severall small parcells of goods, or money... to one person: and that person that receives this Gift, upon the receiving of it goes out, and hollowes thrice for the health and prosperity of the Party that gave it.... (Roger Williams, 1643)

Nickómmo ~ Festival of Nisquanem

This was a solemn ceremony which was held in December during The MOON OF DARKNESS. When the first snow covered the fir trees, the Indians moved from their homes along the ocean back into the forest. They believed that Nisquanem, the Spirit of Mercy, dwelt in the fir trees and that the fir tree would protect them. The ceremony held at this time corresponded in a sense to our Christmas. Every one brought an offering for the less fortunate of the tribe. As they sang and danced in a circle, every one placed the donation of food, totems, leather clothing, amulets, wampum belts and shell beads on the medicine stand. At this time prayers were offered to the Great Spirit for protection from the evil spirits of cold and darkness during the winter season when many of the members passed into the Hereafter. Roger Williams recorded one of these ceremonies, and reports having counted one thousand Indians participating in it. Singing was often extemporaneous. (Princess Red Wing, in Kaiser, p. 7)

There is a modest Religious perswasion not to disturb any man, either themselves *English, Dutch,* or any in their Conscience, and worship, and therfore say: *Peace, hold your peace.* (Roger Williams, 1643)

The Soule

Derived from *Cowwene* to sleep, because say they, it workes and operates when the body sleepes. *Míchachunck* the soule, in a higher notion, which is of affinity, with a word signifying a looking glasse, or clear resemlance, so that it hath its name from a cleere sight or discerning, which indeed seemes very well to suit the nature of it. (Roger Williams, 1643)

They believe that the soules of Men and Women goe to the Souwest, their great and good men and Women to *Cautàntouwit* his House, where they have hopes... of carnall Joyes: Murthers thieves and Lyers, their Soules (say they) wander restlesse abroad. (Roger Williams, 1643)

They apprehending a vast difference of Knowledge between the *English* and themselves, are very observant of the *English* lives: I have heard them say to an Englishman (who being hindred, broke a promise to them). You know God, Will you lie Englishman? (Roger Williams, 1643)

Now the Indian never worshipped anything he could conquer.... (Princess Red Wing, 1986)

The Sky Queen [Algonquian Legend]

Ages ago everybody lived in the sky and down below was all water. And one day the Sky Chief pulled up the great tree of life, and when he did, he made a great hole in the sky and called the Sky Queen to come and look. And when she looked, he gave her a push and down, down she fell and all the little water animals said, "Look! A star is falling. It's the Sky Queen. Where will we put her?" Two great swans came together and caught her on their wings and said, "We can't hold her forever, where will we put her?" Then the old turtle came up from the bottom of the sea and said, "You can put her on my back, but I must have dirt." So all the little water animals went way to the bottom of the sea and brought up a handful of dirt, put it on the turtles' back until it grew. It grew to the East and to the West and to the North and to the South, and the old turtle grew with it. And by and by that turtle was holding up the whole earth.

Now sometimes he gets tired holding up the whole earth and gives himself a shake. People think there having an earthquake, but all the Indian children know that it's just the turtle tired from holding up the earth.

Well by and by they put the Sky Queen down on the earth and after awhile she had two twin sons. One very, very good son and one that was very, very bad. Everything the good son did the evil minded son did something to counteract it. The good minded son made a beautiful sun-shiny day, like today. The evil minded son made it hale, rain, storm, thunder, and to a hurricane. Then the good minded son made a beautiful stream to flow down the hill side, and the evil minded son filled it with snakes, lizards and spiders. Then the good minded son made the beautiful bushes that would burst forth flowers, fruits and berries. He made the trees and the grasses. And the evil-minded son made poison ivy and briars to grow all around.

Well, that poor old lady became so tired trying to separate the good from the evil, that by and by she died. And they put her in the ground.

After a while, from her head grew the pumpkin, from her toes grew the potatoes, from her body grew squash, beans and corn, from her fingers grew the green beans, and ever since that day, Mother Earth has been feeding her children. [traditional]

Geistod—*A New Word in the English Language to Explain American History*

From the German (the language par excellence for these matters), *Geistod* will mean "death of the Spirit." The sole use of the term is for occasions when a word stronger than "genocide" ([physical] death of a race) is required. Geistod refers to a race that has not been physically exterminated but whose Spirit has been annihilated; i.e., a people who have lost their Way. A people to whom Geistod refers is the American Indian. *Geistodology* or *geistodics* will be names of the sciences treating the phenomenon of geistod. (Moondancer, *Neologisms*, 1996)

Wampanoag Prayer

>Great Spirit, I offer this tobacco
>Mother Earth, I offer this tobacco
>Grandmother Moon, I offer this tobacco
>Grandfather Sun, I offer this tobacco
>I thank you
>I offer this tobacco to the four directions
>>to the east
>>to the south
>>to the west
>>to the north
>
>I thank you for all my relations

       the winged nation
       creeping and crawling nation
       the four-legged nation
       the green and growing nation
       and all things living in the water
Honoring the clans
       the deer
       the bear
       the wolf
       the turtle
       the snipe
Great Spirit, I offer this tobacco.

[traditional]

Wampanoag Prayer in Massachusett Langauge

Nuppeântam

Keihtanit, nummag ne wuttamâuog
Ohke, nummag ne wuttamâuog
Okummus nepáuzshad, nummag ne wuttamâuog
Wuttôotchĭkkĭnneasin nippâwus, nummag ne wuttamâuog
Taûbot neanawáyean
Nummag ne wuttamâuog adt yau ut nashik ohke:
    wompanniyeu
    sowanniyeu
    pahtatunniyeu
    nannummiyeu
Taûbot neanawáyean newutche wame netomppauog:
    neg pámunenutcheg
    neg pâmompakecheg
    puppinashimwog
    mehtugquash kah moskehtuash
    namohsog
Quttianumóonk weechinnineummoncheg
    ahtuk
    mosq
    mukquoshim

tunnuppasog
sasasō

Keihtanit, nummag ne wuttamâuog

∞ is an "oo" sound as in "food"
(author's translation)

GOVERNMENT AND JUSTICE

Their government is generally monarchical, their chief sachem or sagamore's will being their law; but yet the sachem hath some chief men, that he consults with as his special counsellors. Among some of the Indians their government is mixed, partly monarchical, and partly aristocratical; their sagamore doing not any weighty matter without the consent of his great men, or petty sagamores. Their sachems have not their men in such subjection, but that very frequently their men will leave them upon distaste or harsh dealing, and go live under other sachems; for that their principal endeavour to carry it obligingly and lovingly unto their people, lest they should desert them, and thereby their strength, power, and tribute would be diminished. (Gookin, 1674, p. 14)

The Massasoit Speech on His Dominion, Naming over 30 Villages

...his men gathered near to him [Massasoit] to whom he turned himself, and made a great speech; they sometimes interposing and, as it were, confirming and applauding him in that he said.... Was not he the Massasoyt, Commander of the country about him: was not such a town his and the people in it? To which they answered These were his and would be at peace with us, and bring them skins to us. After this manner, he named at least thirty places; and their answer was as aforesaid, to every one.... (*Mourt's Relation, 1621*; quoted in Lenz, 1995a, p. 47)

Hobomock, Wampanoag Councilor to The Massasoit, Ousa Mequin: Speaking of the Gravely Ill Massasoit to Edward Winslow, 1623

While you live, you will never see his like again among the Indians; he was not a liar, nor was he bloody and cruel.... From anger he was soon reclaimed; easy to be reconciled toward those who had offended him; his reason was such that he could receive advice from mean men; and he governed his people better with few blows than others did with many... truly loving where he loved... he has ofttimes restrained the malice of the Indians against the English... he is the most faithful friend the English have. (source unknown; quoted in Bonfanti, 1993)

They have an exact forme of King, Priest, and Prophet... their Kings or Governours called *Sachimmaüog*, Kings, and *Atauskowaúg, Rulers*, doe govern: Their Priests, performe and manage their Worship: Their wise men and old men (of which number the Priests are also) whom they call *taupowaüog* they make solemne speeches and Orations, or Lectures to them, concerning Religion, Peace, or Warre and all things. (Roger Williams, 1643)

It is the custome for their Kings to inherite , the sonne always taking the Kingdome after his fathers death. If there be no sonne, then the Queene rules; if no Queene, the next to the blood-royall; who comes in otherwise, is but counted an ursurping intruder, and if his faire carriage beare him not out the better, they will soone unscepter him. (Wm. Wood, 1634; quoted in Trigger, 1978, p. 167)

The *sachims*, although they have an absolute Monarchie over the people; yet they will not conclude of ought that concernes all, either Lawes, or Subsides, or warres, unto which the people are averse, and by gentle perswasion cannot be brought. (Roger Williams, 1643)

Beside their general subjection to the highest *Sachims*, to whome they carry presents: They have also particular Protectors, under *sachims*, to whom they carry presents and upon any injury received, and complaint made, these Protectors will revenge it. (Roger Williams, 1643)

Wampanoag Pineses (Elite Warriors & Counselors)

The *Pineses* are men of great courage and wisdom... and although against their battles, all of them painting, disfigure themselves, yet are they known by their courage and boldness whereof one of them will chase almost a hundred men, for they account it death whomsoever [shall] stand in their way.... They are highly esteemed of all sorts of people and the sachem's Council without whom they will not war or undertake any weighty thing. In war, their Sachems, for their more [added] safety go in the midst of them. They are commonly men of greatest stature and strength and such as will endure most hardness and yet are more discreet, courteous and humane.... And to that end they have many stories of these [Pineses] they train up the most forward and likeliest boys from their childhood in great hardness [ie hardiness] and make them abstain from dainty meat observing divers orders prescribed to the end when they are of age, the Devil may appear to them. Causing to drink the juice of sentry [centaury] and other bitter herbs till they cast [vomit] which them must disgorge into the platter and drink again and again till, at length through extraordinary oppressing of nature it will seem to be all blood. And this the boys will do with eagerness at the first and do continue till, by reason of faintness, they can scarce stand on their legs; and then must go forth in the cold. Also they beat their shins with sticks and cause them to run through bushes, stumps and brambles to make them hardy.... (Edward Winslow, *Good News from New England*, 1624; quoted in Lenz, 1995b, p. 8) [*AUTHOR'S NOTE*: we don't know for certain, but the word *pinese* may mean something like "little bird that moves all about".]

Every Sachem knoweth how far the bounds and limits of his own country extendeth and that is his own proper inheritance. Out of that , if any of his men desire land to set their corn, he giveth them as much as they can use and sets them their bounds. In [within] this circuit whosoever hunteth, if they kill any venison, bringeth him his fee: which is the fore parts of the same, if it be killed on the land; but if [the deer] be killed in the water, then the skin thereof.

Once a year the Pineses use [are accustomed] to provoke the people to bestow much corn on the Sachem. To that end they appoint a certain time and place near the Sachem's dwelling where the people bring ,many baskets of corn.... There the Pineses stand ready to give thanks to the people on the Sachem's behalf and after, acquaineth the Sachem therewith; who fetcheth the same and is no less thankful, bestowing many gifts on them. (Edward Winslow, 1624; quoted in Lenz, 1995b, p. 9)

I could never discerne that excesse of scandalous sins amongst them, which *Europe* aboundeth with.... (Roger Williams, 1643)

... the younger are allwayes obedient unto the elder people, and at their commaunds in every respect without grummling; in all counsels... the younger mens opinion shall be heard, but the old mens opinion and councell imbraced and followed.... (Wm. Wood, 1634; quoted in Lenz, 1995b, pp. 45-46)

In matters of unjust and dishonest dealing the Sachem examineth and punishesth the same. In cases of theft, for the first offence he is disgracefully rebuked; for the second he is beaten by the sachem with a cudgel on the back; for the third he is beaten with many strokes and hath his nose slit upward that all men may both know and shun him. If any man kill another he must likewise for the same.

The sachem not only passeth the sentence upon malefactors; but executeth the same with his own hands, if the party be then present. If not [he] sendeth his own knife, in [a] case of death in the hands of others to perform the same. But if the offended be to receive other punishment he will not receive the same but from the sachem himself; before whom, being naked, he kneeleth and will not offer to run away though to beat him never so much it being a greater disparagement for a man to cry during the time of his correction than is his offence and punishment. (Edward Winslow, *Good News from New England*, 1624; quoted in Lenz, 1995b, p. 10)

MARRIAGE

Whhen a man hath a desire to marry, he first gets the good will of the maid or widow; after the consent of her friends for the part. As for himself, if he at his own disposing, if the king will, the match is made, the dowry of wampompeag paid, the king joins the hands with their hearts, never to part till death.... (Wm Wood, 1634; quoted in Lenz, 1996b, p. 78)

Single fornication they count no sin, but after Mariage (which they solemnize by consent of Parents and publique approbation publiquely) then they count it hainous for either of them to be false. (Roger Williams, 1643)

It hath pleased God in wonderfull manner to moderate that curse of sorrowes of Child-bearing to these poore Indian Women: So that ordinarily they have a wonderfull more speedy and easie Travell [pregnancy], and deliverly then the Women of *Europe*: not that I thinke God is more gracious to them above other Women, but that it followes, First from the hardnesse of their constitution, in which respect they beare their sorrowes easier.

Secondly from their extraordinary great labour (even above the labour of men) as in the Field, they sustaine the labour of it, in carrying mighty Burthens, in digging clammes and getting other Shelfish from the Sea, in beating all their Corne in Morters &c. Most of them count it a shame for a women in Travell to make complaint, and many of them scarcely heard to groane. I have often known in one Quarter of an houre a Woman merry in the House, and delevered and merry again: and within two dayes abroad, and foure or five dayes at worke &c. (Roger Williams, 1643)

Divorce is Common

They put away [divorce] frequently for other ocassions besides Adultery, yet I know many Couples that have lived twenty, thirty, fourty years together. (Roger Williams, 1643)

They Have Many Wives

They take many wives; yet one of them is the principal or chief in their esteem and affection. They also put away [divorce] their wives; and the wives also leave their husbands frequently, upon grounds of displeasure or dissatisfaction. (Gookin, 1674, p. 9)

The Love Signal was also chanted by young braves at this large festival [Harvest Festival, Moon of the Harvest] when so many young men and women met. When a young Indian girl became mature, her father gave a Festival of Pure Maidens every moon until she was chosen to be the mate of some young brave. At the ceremony a large white stone placed in the middle of the Council Fire was sprinkled with blood. The young girl was given an arrow which she placed over her heart with one hand and put the other hand on the stone while she took a vow of purity. Only the pure could participate in this Festival, so all the maidens were anxious to be virtuous so they qualify as the mate for some young brave. At the harvest festival many a pure Indian maiden received the song of love from the lips of an Indian youth. (Princess Red Wing, in Kaiser, p. 4)

It has been said that the Blanket
Is the symbol of Love, Warmth and Sharing to the Native American
And it is for this reason
That The Blanket is given as a Wedding Gift.
       (Traditional; quoted from Tall Oak)

Kumínekes Sq

Peeyantum sent you to me
She smiles on us
I dry the tears that drowned the sun
I can go home—to Mother-Grandmother

Now I can make the talk—from you

We walk together
With our children
Feet Like Thunder—A Great Voice—Little White Flower

The path of nnìnuog

Let it be that way

We are always Strong Woman-Moondancer

K∞womonsh
Kumínekes Sq

[Moondancer]

WAMPUM

Wampum is of two sorts; one white, which they make of the stem of the *Periwincle*, which they call Meteaûhock, when all the shell is broken off: and of this sort... of their small Beads... they make with holes to string the bracelets....

The second is black, inclining to blew, which is made of the shell of a fish, which some *English* call *Hens*, Poquaûhock....

They that live upon the Sea side, generally make of it, and as many make as will. The *Indians* bring all their sorts of Furs, which they take in the Countrey, both to the *Indians* and to the *English* for this *Indian* Money: this Money the *English*, *French* and *Dutch*, trade to the *Indians*, six hundred miles in severall parts (North and South from *New-England*) for their Furres, and wherever they stand in need of from them: as Corne, Venison, &c. (Roger Williams, 1643)

The wompopeague is made artfically of a part of the wilk's [whelks] shell. The black is double value to the white. It is made principally by the Narragansetts block islanders [Indians of Block Island, subjects of Narragansetts; island named after Adrian Block] and long island [Long Island] Indians. Upon the sandy flats and shores of these coasts the wilk shells are found. With this wompompeague they pay tribute, redeem captives, purchase peace with their potent neighbors, as occasion requires; in a word, it answers all occasions with them, as gold and silver doth with us. They delight much in having and using knives, combs, scissors, hatchets, hoes, guns, needles, awls, looking glasses, and such like necessaries, which they purchase of the English and the Dutch with their peague [wampum], and they sell their peltry [animals pelts] for their wampeague [wampum]. (Gookin, 1674, p. 12)

If any murther, or any great wrong upon any of their relatives or kindred, be committed, all of that flock and consanguinity look upon themselves concerned to revenge that wrong, or murder, unless the business be taken up by the payment of wompompeague. (Gookin, 1674, p. 9)

Their white they call *Wompam* [wampum] (which signifies white): their black *Suckáuhock* (*súcki* signifying blacke).... (Roger Williams, 1643)

[*AUTHORS' NOTE*: wampum was a gift of Paumpágussit (Sea Spirit) to the Ancient Ones. The Wampanoag had little of it, and got it in trade. Wampum was not "money" to Indians, since theirs was a trade economy (barter system) and a system of reciprocity or sharing. Europeans turned it into their own idea of money (the black or purple-colored wampum beads were twice as valuable as white beads). Now, Indians used wampum to record their history, declare war & peace & love, as gifts, pay tribute to stronger tribes (like Mafia protection money) as a badge of office by Sachems, and many other uses. The three famous wampum belts of King Philip [probably taken from Annawan (new Massasoit) at Annawon's Rock] are believed to be in England as a war trophy, but we're working for their return with other Wampanoag Indians.]

TRADE

A mongst themselves they trade their Corne, skins, Coates, Venison, Fish, &c and sometimes come ten or twenty in a Company to trade amongst the *English*.
They have some who follow onely making of Bowes, some Arrowes, some Dishes, and (the Women make all their earthen Vessells) some follow fishing, some hunting: most on the Sea-side make [wampum], and store up shells in Summer against Winter whereof to make their [wampum]. (Roger Williams, 1643)

The Indians bring downe all their sorts of Furs, which they take [trap] in the Countrey both to the *Indians* and to the *English* for this Indian money [wampum beads].... [They] trade to the Indians, six hundred miles in severall parts (North and South in *New-England*) for their furres, and whatever they stand in need of from them: as Corne, Venison &c. (Roger Williams, 1643)

They are marvailous subtle in their Bargaines to save a penny: And very suspicious that *English* men labour to deceive them: Therefore they will beate all markets and try all places, and runne twenty, thirty, yea forty mile, and more, and lodge in the Woods, to save six pence. (Roger Williams, 1643)

Elder's View of Effects of Trading with Europeans (1650)

...a long time ago, they [the Indians] had wise men, which in a grave manner taught the people knowledge; but they are dead, and their wisdome is buried with them, and now men live a giddy life, in ignorance, until they are white headed, and though ripe in years, yet they go without wisdome to their graves. (cited in Trigger, p. 88)

HUNTING

The Bow and Arrow

They are trained up to their bows from their childhood; little boys with bows made of little sticks and arrows of great bents will smite down a piece of tobacco pipe every shoot a good way off. As these Indians are good marksmen, so they are well experienced when they very life of every creature lieth, and know where to smite him to make him die presently. (Wm. Wood, 1634; quoted in Lenz, 1995b, p. 82)

More From the Voyages of Italian Explorer Giovanni da Verrazzano, Newport, RI

They live by hunting and fishing, and they are long-lived. If they fall sick, they cure themselves without medicine, by the heat of the fire, and their death at last comes from extreme old age. We judge them to be very affectionate and charitable towards their relatives—making loud lamentations in their adversity, and in their misery calling to mind all their good fortune. At their departure out of life, their relations mutually join in weeping, mingled with singing, for a long time. This is all we could learn of them.... (from *The Voyages of Giovanni da Verrazzano, 1524-1528*; quoted in Lenz, 1994, p. 31)

The Natives hunt two wayes:
    First, when they pursue their game (especially Deere, which is the generall and wonderfull plenteous hunting in the Countrey).

I say, they pursue in twentie, fortie, fiftie, yea, two or three hundred in a company, (as I have seene) when they drive the woods before them.

Secondly, They hunt by traps of severall sorts, to which purpose, after they have observed in Spring-time and Summer the haunt of the Deere, then about Harvest, they goe ten or twentie together, and sometimes more, and withall (if it be not too farre) wives and childrn also, where they build up little hunting houses of Barks and Rushes (not comparable to their dwelling houses) and so each man takes his bounds of two, three, or foure miles, when hee sets thirty, forty, or fiftie Traps, and baits his Traps with the food the Deere loves, and once in two dayes he walks his round to view his traps. (Roger Williams, 1643)

...the Indian makes a falling trap called *sunnúckhig* (with a great weight of stones) and so sometimes knocks the Wolfe on the head.... if it be a black Wolfe [their] skins they greatly prize. (Roger Williams, 1643)

When a Deere (hunted by the Indians, or Wolves) is kild in the water ... this skin is carried to the *Sachim* or Prince, within whose territory the Deere was slaine. (Roger Williams, 1643)

I have seene a Deare [deer] passe by me upon a neck of Land, and a Savage that has pursued him by the view [of footprints or tracks]. I have accompanied him in this pursuite; and the Savage, pricking the Deare, comes where he finds the view [tracks] of two deares together, leading several wayes. One, hee was sure was fresh, but which (by the sence of seeing) he could not judge; therefore, with his knife, hee digs up the other; and smelling to that, concludes it to be the view [track] of the fresh Deare, which hee had pursued; and thereby followes the chase and killes the Deare.... (Thomas Morton, 1632; quoted in Lenz, 1995b, pp. 52-53)

The hunting by the Indians in the old days [before Europeans] was easy for them. They killed animals in proportion as they had need for them. (Nicholas Denys, 1672; quoted in Lenz, 1995c, pp. 161)

Snow Shoes

In winter the hunting was different. Because of the snow, snowshoes were used, by means of which one marches over the snow without sinking in, especially in the morning, because of the freezing at night. (Nicholas Denys, 1672; quoted in Lenz, 1995c, pp. 163)

GAMES

Their Games... are of two sorts; private and publike: Private, and sometime publike; a Game like unto the *English* Cards [called *pium*]; yet, in stead of Cards they play with strong Rushes.

Secondly, they have a kinde of Dice which are Plumb stones painted [3 white and 2 black wooden disks] which they cast in a Tray [and try to guess which color will dominate, white or black], with a mighty noyse [noise] and sweating [game is called *hubhub*]. Their publique *Games* [such as Football] are solemnized with the meeting of hundreds; sometimes thousands.... (Roger Williams, 1643)

The chiefe Gamesters amongst them desire to make their Gods side with them in their Games... therefore I have seene them keepe as a precious stone a piece of Thunderbolt, which is like unto a Crystall, which they dig out of the ground under some tree. Thunder-smitten, and from this stone they have an opinions of successe, and I have not heard any of these prove losers.... (Roger Williams, 1643)

They are addicted to gaming; and will, in that vein, play away all they have. (Gookin, 1674, p. 13)

Keesaqúnnamun, Another kind of solemne publike meeting, wherein they lie under the trees, in a kinde of Religious observation, and have a mixture of Devotions and sports: But their chiefest Idoll of all for sport and game, is (if their land be at peace) toward Harvest, when they set up a long house called *Qunnèkamuck*. Which signifies *Longhouse*, sometimes an hundred, sometimes two hundred foot long upon a plaine neer the Court (which they call *Kitteickaúick*) where many thousands, men and women meet, where he that goes in danceth in the sight of all the rest; and is prepared for money, coats, small breeches, knifes, or what hee is able to reach to, and gives these things away to the poore, who yest must particularly beg and say, *Cowequetúmmous*, that is, I *beseech you;* which word (although there is not one common beggar amongst them) yet they will often use when their richest amongst them would fain obtain ought by gift. (Roger Williams, 1643)

WAR

If it be in time of *warre*, he that is a *Messenger* runs swiftly, and at every towne the *Messenger* comes, a fresh *Messenger* is sent: he that is the last, comming within a mile or two of the Court, or chiefe house, he *hollowes* often, and they that heare answer him, until by mutuall *hollowing* and answering hee is brought to the place of *audience*, where by this meanes is gathered a great confluence of people to entertain the *newes*. (Roger Williams, 1643)

Their Weapons are Bows and Arrows

Their weapons heretofore were bows and arrows, clubs, and tomahawks, made of wood like a pole axe, with a sharpened stone fastened therein, and for defense, they had targets made of barks of trees.... (Gookin, 1674, p. 12)

Carry Back Heads on Wooden Spears

Their people use no other weapons in war than bows and arrows, saving that their captains have long spears on which, if they return conquerors, they carry the heads of their chief enemies that they slay in the wars, it being their custom to cut off their heads, hands and feet to bear home to their wives and children as true tokens of their renowned victory. (Wm. Wood, 1634, quoted in Lenz, 1995b, p. 81)

Indian Warfare is Different Than European Style

When they go to their wars, it is their custom to paint their faces with diversity of colors, some being all black as jet, some red, some half red and half black, some black and white, others spotted with diverse kinds of colors, being all disguised to their enemies to make them more terrible to their foes, putting likewise their rich jewels, pendants, and wampompeag, to put them mind they fight not only for their children, wives, and lives, but likewise for their goods, lands, and liberties. Being thus armed with this warlike paint, the antic warriors make towards their enemies in a disordered manner, without any soldierlike marching or warlike posture, being deaf to any word of command, ignorant of falling off or falling on, of doubling ranks or files, but let fly their winged shaftments without being fear to wit. Their artillery being spent, he that hath no more arms to fight, finds legs to run away. (Wm. Wood, 1634; quoted in Bragdon, 1996, p. 223)

The men, in their wars, do use turkey or eagle's feathers stuck in their hair, as it is traced up in a roll. Others wear deer shuts, made up in the fashion of a cock's comb died [dyed] red, crossing their heads like a half moon. (Gookin, 1674, p. 13)

War Dance [Mattwakaonk]

They use great vehemency in the motion of their bodies, in their dances; and sometimes the men dance in greater numbers in their war dance. (Gookin, 1674, p. 13)

Their warres are far less bloudy and devouring then the cruell Warres of *Europe;* and seldome slaine in a pitch field: partly because when they fight in a wood every Tree is a Bucklar [hide behind for protection].

When they fight in a plaine, they fight with leaping and dancing, that seldome an Arrow hits, and when a man is wounded, unlesse he that shot followes upon the wounded, they soone retire and save the wounded: and yet having no Swords, nor Guns, all that are slain are commonly slain with great valour and Courage: for Conquerour ventures into the thickest, and brings away the Head of his Enemy. (Roger Williams, 1643)

Timequássin to cut off, or behead, which they are most skilfull to do in a fight; for when they wound, and their arrow sticks in the body of their enemy... in the twinkling of an eye fetch off his head though but with a sorry knife. (Roger Williams 1643)

They are much delighted after battell to hang up the heads and hands of their enemies.... (Roger Williams, 1643)

SICKNESS

When any are visited with sickness, their friends resort unto them for their comfort and continue with them oft times till their death, or recovery. (Edward Winslow, 1624; quoted in Lenz, 1995b, p. 9)

Sweatlodge [pésuponck]

This Hot-house is a kind of little Cell or cave, six or eight foot over, round, made on the side of a hill (commonly by some Rivulet or Brooke) into this frequently the men enter after they have exceedingly heated it with store of wood, laid upon an heape of stones in the midle. When they have taken out the fire, the stones keepe still a great heat: Ten, twelve, twenty. more or lesse, enter at once starke naked, leaving their coats, small breeches (or aprons) at the doore, with one to keepe all: here doe they sit round these hot stones an houre or more, taking *Tobacco*, discoursing, and sweating together; which sweating they use for two ends: First, to cleanse their skin: Secondly, to purge their bodies, which doublesse is a great means of preserving them, and recovering from diseases... which by sweating and some potions, they perfectly and speedily cure: when they come forth (which is matter of admiration) I have seene then runne (Summer and Winter) into the Brooks to coole them, without the least hurt. (Roger Williams, 1643)

DEATH AND BURIAL

I f they die, they stay a certain time to mourn for them. Night and morning they perform this duty many days after the burial in a most doleful manner; insomuch as though it be ordinary and the note musical which they take one from another and all together; yet it will draw tears from their eyes and almost ours also. (Winslow, 1624; quoted in Lenz, 1995b, p. 9)

They Are so Emotional & Strongly Attached to Their Loved Ones— Living & Dead

Which bewailing is very solemne amongst them morning and evening, and sometimes in the night they bewaile their lost husbands, wives, children, brethren or sisters, &c. Sometimes a quarter, halfe, yea, a whole yeere, and longer, if it be for a great Prince.

In this time (unlesse a dispensation be given) they count it a profane thing either to play (as they much use to doe) or to paint themselves, for beauty, but for mourning; or to be angry, and fall out with any, &c. (Roger Williams, 1643)

If it be the man or woman of the house, they will pull down the mats, and leave the frame standing, and bury them in or near the same, and either remove their dwelling or give over house-keeping. (from Winslow; quoted in Bragdon, 1996, p. 198)

He is in Blacke

That is, he hath some dead in his house (whether wife or child &c.) for although at the first being sicke, all the Women and Maides blacke their faces with soote and other blackings; yet upon the death of the sicke, the father, or husband, and all his neighbors, the men also... weare blacke *Faces*, and lay on soote very thicke, which I have often seene clotted with their tears.

This blacking and lamenting they observe in mist dolefull manner, divers weekes and monthes; yea, a yeere if the person be great and publike. (Roger Williams, 1643)

The women in the times of their mourning, after the death of their husbands or kindred,do paint their faces all over black, like a negro; and so continue in this posture many days. (Gookin, 1674, p. 13)

When they bury the dead, they sew up the corpse in a mat, and so put it in the earth. If the party be a sachim, they cover him with many curious mats, and bury all his riches with him, and enclose the grave with pale. If it be a child, the father will also put his own most special jewels and ornaments in the earth with it; also will cut his hair, and disfigure himself very much, in token of sorrow. (*Mourt's Relation*, 1622; quoted in Bragdon, 1996, p. 234)

When they come to the Grave, they lay the dead by the Grave's mouth, and then all sit downe and lament,that I have seen teares run down the cheekes of stoutest Captaines.... [Sachim] *Caunounicus*, having buried his sonne, he burn'd his own Palace, and the goods in it ... in a sollemne remembrance of his sonne, and in a kind of humble Expiation to their Gods, who (as they believe) had taken his sonne from him. (Roger Williams, 1643)

As they abound in lamentations for the dead, so they abound in consolation to the living, and visit them frequently, using this word *Kutchimmoké, Kutchimmoké*, Be of good cheere, which they express by stroaking the cheeke and head of the father or mother, husband, or wife of the dead. (Roger Williams, 1643)

They abhorre to mention the dead by name, and therefore, if any man beare the name of the dead he changeth his name; and if any stranger accidently name him, he is checkt, and if any wilfully name him he is fined; and amongst States, the naming of their dead *Sachims*, is one ground of their warres.... (Roger Williams, 1643)

Inscription Copied from a Grave Stone at Gay Head, Martha's Vineyard, Written in Massachusett Language (Numbers over words are a key for explanation below)

$$\overset{1}{\text{YEUUH}} \quad \overset{2}{\text{WOHHOK}} \quad \overset{3}{\text{SIPSIN}} \quad \overset{4}{\text{SIL PAUL}}$$

$$\overset{5}{\text{NOHTOBEYONTOK}} \quad \text{AGED 49 YEARS}$$

$$\overset{6}{\text{NUPPOOP}} \quad \overset{7}{\text{TAH}} \quad \text{AUGUST 24, 1787}$$

English Explanation:

1. Here
2. The body
3. Lies
4. Sil(as) Paul
5. An ordained preacher   Aged 49 years
6. Died
7. On August 24, 1787.

APPENDIX I

CONTRIBUTIONS OF THE NEW ENGLAND INDIANS TO AMERICA

A reprint of a brochure prepared by the Council as part of *The Wampanoag Indian Exhibit*, held at The Newport Public Library in RI in celebration of Native American Heritage Month, Nov., 1997.

Our culture is deeply indebted to the native peoples of our country. In New England and elsewhere on Turtle Island (all of the United States of America) the American Indian has contributed many things and concepts that most of us are not even aware of. There is hardly anything that one can do, hardly anywhere that one can go which does not involve the influence of the native peoples who have lived here for thousands of years. The contributions, influences and legacies of the Indians can be seen in all aspects of our lives, and all over the continent of America—from government, child rearing, warfare, clothing, to the foods we eat.

We will share with you a small sampling of the contributions of the Indians in New England and elsewhere.

GOVERNMENT: The first concepts of a true participatory democracy, reflected in our Constitution and Bill of Rights, come from the influence of Indian democratic government, attested by the United States Congress.

MILITARY: Guerrilla warfare tactics were learned first from New England Indians in the 1600s. The Quonset hut is based on the Indian Longhouse. We name our weapon systems after Indians: Apache Helicopter, Tomahawk Missile, etc. Paratroopers yell "Geronimo" when they jump out of planes. In W.W. II we used the Navaho and other languages to encode messages.

CONSERVATION: We're turning more and more to Indian concepts of land conservation and the precept of Indian's respect for the land ("Take only what you need and no more") to help us combat problems of pollution, the disappearance of the wilderness, overcrowding.

CHILD REARING: The international Boy Scouts and Girl Scouts movements were based on Indian lifestyle. The Indian practice of group-oriented decision making influences our rearing of children.

INDIAN DEVICES: To mention a few—wigwams, canoes & kayaks, snowshoes & dogsleds, toboggans, hammocks, ponchos & parkas, smoking pipes, rubber syringes, moccasins, tomahawks, and so on. People wear Indian jewelry and have Indian designs on their clothing, bed and beach blankets. Teenagers are great emulators of Indian warriors with their Mohawk haircuts and leather, fringed clothing.

FOOD AND RELATED: Corn, popcorn, beans, potatoes, squash, succotash, Indian tobacco, Johnny Cake, hominy, clambakes, quahogs, maple syrup & sugar, are a few delicacies we still enjoy today. Fish fertilizer is still used in farming in the manner taught by the Wampanoag Indians. And the scarecrow is still scaring away unwanted birds from our farmers' crops just as the early settlers learned from the Wampanoag Indians.

MEDICINE AND RELATED: Herbal remedies and teas, pain relievers, laxatives, muscle relaxants, and other medicines, not to mention ingredients in mouthwash and chewing gum, come from our Indian ancestors throughout Turtle Island.

ANIMAL NAMES: Skunk, moose, chipmunk, raccoon, woodchuck, opossum, muskrat are all New England Algonquian names.

PLACE NAMES AND RELATED: Thousands of names for states, cities, towns, streets, schools, businesses, parks, rivers, lakes, mountains in our country bear Indian names. We name our automobiles, sports teams, beers and other things after Indians throughout Turtle Island.

MISCELLANEOUS: We can mention—
* that many of our major highways and byways in New England are old Indian trails.
* that many of our New England farms are old Indian villages & corn fields.
* American Indians volunteer for military service at a higher rate than any other segment of the population.
* the first Thanksgiving in America took place in Plymouth, Massachusetts in 1621. Your history books do not tell you this, but it was the Wampanoag Indians who suggested to Governor Bradford in 1621 that it is better to thank your God for what you do have rather than lamenting what you do not

have—and that is distinctly the Indian spiritual way.
* the rubber ball, and games of lacrosse and baseball are Indian-based.
* "Rock-a-Bye-Baby" is still sung across America, just the way it was learned from Wampanoag Indians many years ago in Colonial times
* In everyday speech we use words and phrases that come from the ancient Indians, such as—papoose, wampum, pow wow, Big Chief, sachem, sagamore, brave, squaw, thunder bird, bury the hatchet, smoke the peace pipe, run the gauntlet, you speak with forked tongue, fire water, fly (talk) straight as an arrow, Indian file, scalp, war paint & war path, smoke signal, Indian Summer, Indian pony, Indian paint brush, Indian time, Indian giver, War Bonnet, happy hunting ground, a feather in your cap, and others you can mention
* many people are embracing the Indian philosophy of love of nature and family, balance & harmony in life, rather than a love of material objects.
* We do not have the space to mention the influences of Indians to the areas of art, literature, television and cinema, dance, and so many more areas.

INDIAN CHARACTER (Historical Quotes Of 1600s):

"... they are not of a dumpish, sad nature, but rather naturally cheerful."

"... seldom are their words and their deeds strangers .... "

"Whomever commeth in when they are eating, they offer them to eat of that which they are eating ...."

"Such is their love for one another that they cannot endure to see their countrymen wronged, but will stand stiffly in their defense, plead strongly in their behalf ...."

"There are no beggars amongst them, nor fatherlesse children unprovided for. "

"Their affections, especially to their children, are very strong; so that I have knowne a Father take so grievously the losse of his childe, that he hath cut and stob'd himselfe with griefe and rage."

"Such is their mild temper of their spirits that they cannot endure objurgations or scolding."

"The younger sort reverence the elder ...."

"Commonly they never shut their doores, day nor night; and 'tis rare that any hurt is done."

"They are full of businesse, and as impatient of hinderance (in their kind) as any Merchant in Europe."

"Many of them naturally Princes, or else industrious persons, are rich; and the poore amongst them will say, they want nothing."

"Their warres are far less bloudy and devouring then the cruell Warres of Europe; and seldome slaine in a pitcht field .... "

"[In] many ways hath their advice and endeavor been advantageous unto us [the English], they being our instructors for the planting of their Indian corn, by teaching us to cull out the finest seed, to observe the fittest season, to keep distance for holes and fit measure for hills, to worm and weed it, to prune it, and dress it as occasion shall require."

Thus, the debt we owe to the native people of New England and all over this land is enormous. The Wampanoag Indians of Rhode Island and Massachusetts greeted you, and taught and nurtured you when you came to these rocky shores over 377 years—cold, hungry and tired. Without us, you would have surely perished.... The Indian still has something to give to this great land of ours!

APPENDIX II

TRANSLATION OF SOME INDIAN PLACE NAMES IN SOUTHERN NEW ENGLAND

A Note on Translations

The place names in this appendix are based on several, but related, Algonquian languages of southern New England. The method of translating the old Indian names into English involves several steps. We proceed from the linguistic level (what do the roots mean?).

Let's illustrate with the name for the Massachusetts town *Mattapoisett*, meaning (in the author's interpretation) "little resting place". The *first* step involves dividing up the given word into elements that might correspond to the basic meanings of the word (prefixes, roots, suffixes). We decide on two elements for now: "mattapo-isett". *Now*, using knowledge of the Wampanoag language called Massachusett, we recognize that the word-part "mattapo" probably comes from *mattappu* = "he sits down" (or) "he rests" (Moondancer, Strong Woman, 1996). *Next* we see that the element "isett" is probably two elements (is-ett) that come from -*es* = "little" and -*et* = "place of, at, near". *Thus*, putting it all together, we assemble the primary root elements, *mattappu-es-et*. In the *final* step (pronunciation), we contract the elements to obtain something like, *mattappuset* = "he rests + little + place of" or just "little resting place". This is probably how Wampanoag Indians called this place, which in the mouths of the English, was corrupted to Mattapoisett (see Appendix VI for Pronunciation Guide). The following chart summarizes what we just said.

Thus the modern place name Mattapoisett is fairly close to the

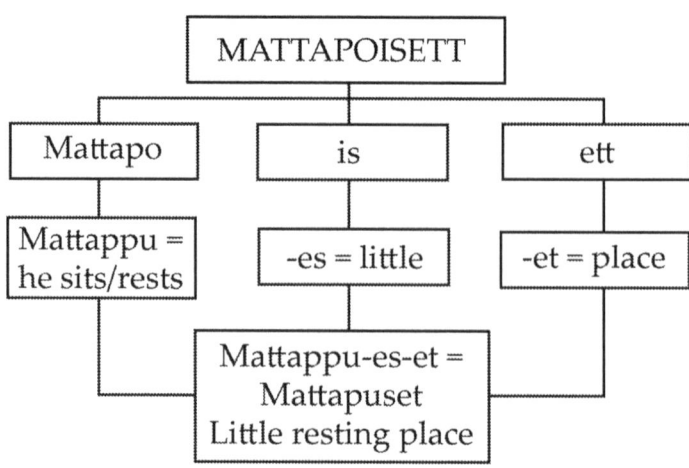

original Algonquian roots and not much seems to be lost in the translation. This is not always the case.

The next page gives another chart-analysis for the place in Massachusetts called *Swampscott*, meaning "at the red rock", or "red rock place".

The analysis for Swampscott demonstrates that many, many old Indian place names were corrupted (sometimes beyond recognition) by the Europeans. To illustrate this problem, one well-known Algonquian translator has said of the place names in Rhode Island, that one-half of them defy analysis altogether! This fact shows why in the tables below you will sometimes see more than one meaning for a name. Different assumptions about the correct Algonquian roots led to different conclusions.

As mentioned, the last step in translation involves contracting or abbreviating the primary root elements. Now, Algonquian languages are described as being *polysynthetic*, meaning that many simple elements or roots are combined into a single word involving final contraction or abbreviation of the primary roots. For example, to say "a white man" we pick our primary elements from the Massachsuett language: *wompesu* = "(he is) white" (animate objects) + *wosketomp* = "a man (young warrior?)". The final word is *womposketomp* = "a white man". Can you see what was contracted in the primary terms? The ability to form the right word through polysynthetic analysis requires knowledge of the correct syntax rule (hundreds exist). These rules (and Indian languages in general) continue to defy the best minds in linguistics!

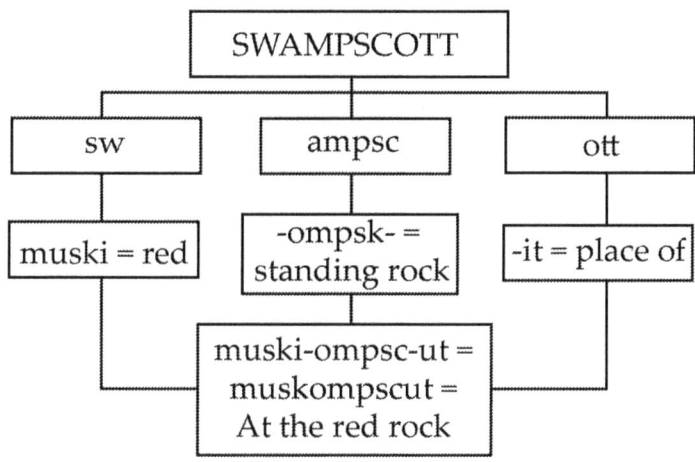

The following list of roots can be used in deciphering some of the Indian place names in the rest of this Appendix. The first column gives roots in the original Indian language, the second shows alternative corrupted spellings seen in the actual names, and lastly, the meaning of the Algonquian. Translations begin by searching for the corrupted fragments. Examples shown at end of the lists.

List of Some Roots for Translation Assistance
(Source: Trumbull, 1881 and Authors)

I. Land Names

Algonquian	Modern (corrupted) Spelling	Meaning
-adene	-ahdin, -ahd, -attiny	hill, mountain
-komuk	comuc, -commuck, -gomuck	enclosed/limited place
munnoh, munnohan	munna, manha, minna, menhan, munhan	island
munnoh-es	munnisses, manises, minis	little island
naïag	niack, nyack, nayaug, nawayack, naïänk, nahig, nanhig, narrag	a point of land
ohke, auke	ac, ack, aug, auc, ag, ic, ick, ik, ahki, ocke, ock, oc, ogue, uc	land, ground, place
-ompsk	obsk, -mpsk, -msk, -ms, -psk, -pisk	a standing or upright rock
-'tuck	-tuck, -tunk, -tak	wood, tree
-unk	-onk	a standing tree
wadchu, wauchu-adchu	watchu, wachu, achu, choo, chu	hill, mountain

II. Water Names

Algonquian	Modern (corrupted) Spelling	Meaning
-amaug	-amag, -amock, -ameock, -ameugg, -amyock, -amareck, -amelake, -amuck, -amond	fishing-place
-paug	-pog, -poge, -pogue, -pauk, -pawog, -baug, -bog, -pag, -pague, -bogue	pond, lake
-pauges, -paugeset	-paugset, -pogset, -poxet, -boxet, -boxy	little pond, lake
-pe (for nippe)	-pi, -bi	fresh water for drinking
-pe-auke	-peag, -piak, -piac, -bequi, -bec	water-land, water-place
pauntuck	pawtuck, powntuck, poountuck, patuck	water falls in a tidal river
pauntuk-ese		small water falls in a tidal river
sauk	-suc, -suck, -sauga, -saco, -sag, -sague, -seogee	outlet of a river or brook, stream flowing out of a pond or lake
sepu, seip	sip, sippi, sep, seppe	a long river
sepu-es	sepose, sepo, sebese, sebethe	a short river
-tuck-es	-tucks, -tux, -tuxet	a small tidal or broad river, estuary
-tuk	-tick, -tic, *etc.*	a tidal or broad river, estuary

III. Adjectives & Descriptives

Algonquian	Modern (corrupted) Spelling	Meaning
chepi-	chippi-, chabe-, chappa-, chaub-	separated, apart
kehti-, kehchi-	keht-, kehte-, ket-, kit-, kut-, cot-, cat-, kt-, te-, tit-	chief, principal, greatest
matchi-, mache-	mat-, maut-, matta-	bad, evil, unpleasant, unfavorable
missi-, mishe-, massa-	massa-, mis-, mashe, mas-, moshe-, mus-, she-	great, big
nashaui	nashawe, nashaway, natchaw, naush, ashwa, show, showa, shew, she	midway, between
nuppis, nips	nawbes	little water, a small pond, lake
ogguhse-, ogkosse-	oxo-, oxy-, abscu-	small, little
ogkome	accom-, agame-	on the other side of, over against
ongkoue	uncoa, uncawa, uncoway, unqua	beyond
pohque	pohqua-, pauqua-, paqua- payqua-, pequa-, poqua-, poco-, pyqua-, puckwa-, pahcu-, pughquo-	clear, open (as land)
pohqu'un	poquon-, pocon-, paquan- pequon-, pecon-	cleared, opened (as land)
pohquettah-un	poquetan-, paucutun-, pogatan-, pocotan-, cod-dan-, cuttyhun-, cotting-	broken-up, cultivated
sonki	soonka, sunki, saunquo, songi	cool to touch, taste
weque-, wequa-	weca-, wico-, ukwe-, aquee-, aqua-	at the end of
wongun	wongum, wangom	crooked, bent, winding
wunni-, winni-	wirri-, wera-, willi-, waure-	good, easy, pleasing, favorable

IV. Plurals & Locatives (Location)

Algonquian	Modern (corrupted) Spelling	Meaning
-ash	-ass	many, much of (plural ending)
-et, -ut, -it	-at, -chet, -itt	at, in, near, place of (word ending)
-es, -is	-ese, -as, -us	little, small (ending of word)
-og	-aog, -ug, -ag, -ig	many, much of (plural ending)
-set, -eset	-sett, -sets, -eset, -setts, -esets	little place of (word ending)

EXAMPLES

Massachusetts = massa + wadchu + ash + et (place of big hills)
Narragansett = naiag + es + et (place of narrow small point)
Massaco = massa + sauk (great outlet)
Norwalk = nay + aug (a point of land)
Warwick **NOT INDIAN NAME** even though "war", "ick" may appear to be roots. People make this mistake often. That shows just how mangled the words are in the records.

For other examples, see

Roger Williams (1643)
Huden (1962)
Masthay (1987)
O'Brien (2003)

HISTORIC SOUTHERN NEW ENGLAND NATIONS, TRIBES, VILLAGES

NAME[1]	TRANSLATION
Accomack	on the other side
Accominta	beyond the little river
Agawam	low land; overflowed by water; an unloading place
Amagansett	—at the council place where we smoke, —at the fishing place, at the point
Amoskeag	fishing place
Aquidneck	at the island, suspended floating mass
Aquinnah (Gay Head)	peace camp
Ashquoash	green garden stuff
Assonet	at the rock place
Chabanakongkomun, Chabanakongmuk	boundary fishing place
Corchaug	?
Coweset	place of young pine trees
Hammonesset	at place of small islands or sandbars
Hassanamesit	small stones place
Hoosic	kettle rim; writing house?
Housatonic	beyond the mountain
Kenunckapacoof, Kenuck Pacooke	where the body of the water bends or turns
Magunkaquog	place of the gift
Mahican, Mohican	wolf
Manchage	place of departure or marveling

1. The source for most of the translations is Huden (1962). Some names have been translated or re-translated by the authors. Gookin (1674) provided some in Massachusetts, including Cape Cod and the Islands. A number of other tribal names (not translated) may be found in the book by Bragdon, 1996, pp. 20-25.

Mashpee	land near the great cove; large pond
Massachusett	near the great hills
Massacoe, Massaco, Massaqua, Mussawco, Massacowe, Mushko	great land; outlet
Mattapoisett	little resting place
Menameset	at the place where fish abound
Menunkatuck, Menuckketuck, Menunquatuck, Menunketesuck	strong flowing stream
Mohegan	wolf people
Montauk, Munnawtawkit	at the fort; high land (fort place)
Montup, Montaup, Montop	lookout place (Massasoit's Village)
Narragansett	at the small narrow point (Nahicans = Narragansetts)
Nashoba	between waters
Natick	my home, my land (place where Massachusett language recorded by Indians and missionary John Eliot)
Naugatuck	one tree
Naumkeag	eel place
Nauset, Nawset	at the place between (Cape Cod Bay and Atlantic Ocean); on the point
Nehantic, Niantic	point of land on a tidal river or estuary
Neponset	a good (or easy) waterfall
Niantic	people of the point
Nipmuck, Nipnet	fresh water fishermen
Nonotuck	narrow river; in the middle of the river
Nowass, Nawass	between rivers; at the point
Norwottuck	place far from us
Pamet, Pawmet, Paumet	wading place; at the shallow cove
Paquoag	open or clear place
Pascataway	where the river divides
Paugusset	-swift current in the divided river -river widens out -where the fork joins -small pond place

Pawtucket	at the water falls
Pawtuxet, Pautuxet, Patuxet	at the little falls (first Plymouth Village of Pilgrims; an old Indian village destroyed by epidemic). [Pautuxet was called Ompaan by Indians in King Philip's War (see B. Church, 1716)]
Pennacook	at the foothills; sloping down place
Pequot	destroyers
Peskeompscut	at the split rocks
Pocasset	where the stream widens
Pocumtuck	narrow swift river
Podunk	where you sink in (imitative sound)
Pokanoket, Pawkunnawkutt	at the cleared land [a tribal territory of Massasoit Ousa Mequin's home; Pokanoket was used by English to mean all Wampanoag peoples]
Pomperaug	place to walk, play; rocky place
Poquonock	cleared land (for cultivation)
Potatuck, Powtatuck	land near the (water) falls
Punkapog	shallow fresh water pond
Quabaug	beyond the pond
Quinebaug	long pond
Quinnatukut (Connecticut)	long tidal river
Quinnipiac, Quillipeak, Quillipeag, Quillipiac, Quinopiock, Quinnypiock	place where the path changes direction, course
Quiripi	where we change our route
Sagkonet, Saconet, Sakonett	black goose abode; rock outlet; at the outlet
Schaghticoke, Scatacook, Scaticook, Skaticook	where two rivers come together or divide
Seekonk, Seaconke	— black goose place (Native American translation), — an outlet; mouth of the stream
Senecksig, Senexit	place of small stones
Shawmut (Boston and surroundings & Wampanoag village)	— at the neck (where we pull up our canoes), — canoe landing place
Shinnecock	place of stone?

Sicaog (Hartford, CT)	dark earth; muddy place
Sickanames	black fish
Siwanog	south people (probably)
Siwanoy	south people
Sokonnesset, Sockanosset	place of dark colored earth
Sowams	the south country (Narragansett name for Pokanoket)
Sowheage, Sequin	southland, south Sachemdom
Squakheag	watching place; spearing fish
Swampscott	at the red rock
Tunxis	fast flowing and winding stream
Unquachog	?
Wabaquasset	place where we make mats for house coverings
Wamesit	there is room for all
Wampanoag	people of the first light
Wangunk	crooked land?
Wappinger	easterners
Waramaug, Werewaug	good fishing place
Wauchimoqut	end of fishing place
Weantinaug, Weantinoque, Weantinock, Weantinoque, Wiantenuck, Wyantenug	where the river swirls or tumbles around a hill
Weekapaug	at the end of the pond
Wepaweaug	narrows; crossing place
Weshakim	surface of sea
Wessagusset	at the edge of the rocks
Woronoco	winding about
Wuttapa, Watuppa	roots (for sewing); where we sit and talk

RESERVATIONS AND SETTLEMENTS AND OTHER PLACES

State of Massachusetts
(excluding Cape Cod or Nauset)

NAME[2]	TRANSLATION
Acushnet	at the cove
Annawomscutt	at the shell rock; Annawon's Rock
Annawon	commander or conqueror (name of Wampanoag missinnige or War Chief in King Phillip's war)
Assameskq	a cave
Assonet	at the rock place
Assowamsoo, Assowamset	halfway place
Chabanakongkomun, Chabanakongmuk	boundary fishing place
Chickatawbut	his wetu (house) is on fire
Coaxit, Coxit, Coquitt (Part of Dartmouth)	an arrow point; at the high point
Cokesit	pine place
Copicut	at the refuge place
Cotuhtikut	planting fields place
Hassanamesit	small stones place
Hassanamisco	small stones place
Hobbomock	evil spirit
Horseneck	a cave; cavern; rock shelter
Magunkaquog	place of the gift
Manchage	place of departure or marveling

2. Some names are repeated from other sections (e.g., Assonet) so that the reader will know the meaning of the name in different contexts and have flexibility in locating a name under different headings. Also some names listed by State cross multiple States. Famous Wampanoag names like Mashpee are listed under **Nations, Tribes, Villages**.

Massachusetts	near the great hills
Mattakesit	black mud place
Merrimack	deep place
Monimoint	deep black mire?
Nanepashemet	he walks the night (Moon Sachem)
Nashaway	between two river branches
Nashobah	between waters
Nashua	between streams
Natick	my home, my land (place where Massachusett language recorded by Indians and missionary John Eliot)
Nauset, Nawset	at the place between (Cape Cod Bay and Atlantic Ocean); on the point
Nonantum	I am glad, I rejoice
Nukkehkummees	small shelter
Okommakamesit	at the field other side
Ompaan, Umpame, Ampame	— resting place? — turn around or back (resurrect this village?) [first Plymouth Village of Pilgrims; an old Indian village called Pautuxet; destroyed by epidemic. When English occupied, called Ompaan by Indians in King Philip's War (see B. Church, 1716)]
Pakachoog	turning place?
Punkapog	shallow fresh water pond
Quabaug	beyond the pond
Quittacus	red rock; long brook
Sagus	the outlet; small outlet
Seekonk, Seaconke	black goose place; an outlet; mouth of the stream
Shawmut (Boston and surroundings & Wampanoag village)	— at the neck (where we pull up our canoes); — canoe landing place
Somerset, Samerset	named after Samoset, a sagamore of Abenaki Indians who first greeted the Pilgrims in March, 1621

Squannacook	—salmon place; —in the seasdon of the gardens or green place
Squantum	a door or gate; angry god (place of?)
Swampscott	at the red rock
Titicut (Tauton)	the principal river
Tittituck (Blackstone River)	the great or principal river
Wachuset	small mountain place
Waeuntug	good tidal stream?; winding stream?
Wamesit	there is room for all
Wannamoisett	at the good fishing place
Watchimoquet, Watchimoquit, Watchemoket	end of fishing place or cove
Watuppa	roots (for sewing); where we sit and talk
Wawayontat,Weweanteit (Wareham)	winding creek
Weetomoe	the wetu (lodge) keeper (name of famous Squaw Sachem of Pocassets)
Weshakim	surface of sea
Weweantic	crokked stream
Woronke	winding about place
Wunnashowatukqut (Blackstone R.)	where the river divides

RESERVATIONS AND SETTLEMENTS AND OTHER PLACES

Cape Cod

NAME[3]	TRANSLATION
Ashumet	pond at the spring
Ashimuit	at the spring
Assoowaamsoo, Assoowamset (part of Middleborough)	—the half-way place; —half-way to southwest; —other side of Sowams (south country)
Coatuit, Cotuit	—at the pine tree place; —at the long planting fields
Codtanmut	—deserted place; —trading place; —where they sing
Comassakumkanit	at the rock which stands erect
Cotuhtikut, Titicut (part of Middleborough)	at the great tidal river
Hyannis	he [Sachem Iannough] wages war
Kitteaumut, Katamet (Sandwich or Buzzard's Bay)	principal fishing place
Manamoyik (Chatham)	carry or burden place
Mannamit (sandwich, bottom of Buzzard's Bay)	where they carry burdens on their backs
Mashpee	land near the great cove; large pond
Matakees (Barnstable & Yarmouth harbors)	big meadow; little trees
Mattapoisett	little resting place
Meeshawn	—a landing place; —ferry (he goes by boat, place of); —great land neck

3. Some information taken from Gookin (1674). See also under **Nations, Tribes, Villages**.

Monomoy Island	— lookout place; deep water
Nantucket	— place in the middle of the water; — at far off sea-place; — where it is, the sea gets broader; — far off among the waves; — point of land in the middle; — narrow river
Nausett, Nawset (north part of Eastham)	at the place between (Cape Cod Bay and Atlantic Ocean); on the point
Nobsquassit (N. East part of Yarmouth)	at the rock ledge cliff
Pawpoesit (within Town of Mashpee)	— snipe (or partridge) country; — at the little place
Pispogutt	at the miry pond
Popponesset	—at the frost fish or tomcod fishing place; —place of obstructed outlet; —lookout place
Potanumaquut (S. East Eastham)	foaming island place
Punonakanit	— out of the way beach; — distant enclosure
Quashnet	at the small cove
Saconeset, Sokones (Falmouth)	dark earth
Satuit	— cold brook; — salt (or cold) stream
Sawkattukett (West part of Harwich)	at the outlet of the tidal creek
Setucket	at the mouth of the tidal river
Shumuit	at the spring of good water
Sokones	dark earth
Wakoquet, Waquoit (within Town of Mashpee)	house place
Waquoit	at the end (of the bay)
Wawayontat, Wewewanteit (Wareham), Weequakut, Chechwacket	place at the end
Weesquobs	shining rocks

RESERVATIONS AND SETTLEMENTS AND OTHER PLACES

The Islands
(Block Island, Martha's [Martin's] Vineyard, Nantucket, Elizabeth Islands, Chappaquidick Island)

NAME[4]	TRANSLATION
Aquinnah (Gay Head)	peace camp
Chappaquiddick	at the separated island
Manisses, Manissean (Block Island)	—little island; —little god (place of?)
Nantucket	—place in the middle of the water; —at far off sea-place; —where it is, the sea gets broader; —far off among the waves; —point of land in the middle; —narrow river
Nashuakemmiuk	middle of dark land
Nope (Martin's or Martha's Vineyard)	menhaden fish place
Nunnepoag	fresh or narrow pond
Oggawame, Agawam	—low land; —overflowed by water; —an unloading place
Ohkatomka	top of the rock
Pacamkik	—abode of codfish (Haddock?); —dark land (well fertilized); —open land
Peschameeset	—where we catch & split small fish; —blue place?
Seconchqut	at the summer place
Sengekontakit	at cold, long creek
Squatesit	red place or brook
Talhanio	low meadow
Toikiming (Christiantown)	at the mill or rushing spring
Wammasquid	at the plain

4. See also under **Nations, Tribes, Villages.**

OTHER NAMES

State of Rhode Island

NAME[5]	TRANSLATION
Aguspemokick (Gould's Island)	short scant narrows
Apponaug	where he roasts oysters
Aquidneck	at the island
Awashonks	woman who rules (name of famous Squaw Sachem of Sagkonates in Little Compton, RI)
Bassaqutogaug	where trees were split?
Cawncawnjawatchuk	very long hill
Cawsumsett	sharp rock place
Chabatawece	little separated place
Chachacust	at the small widening out place?
Chachapacassett	at or near the great widening
Chagum	—a black bird; surface of the sea; —the great provider?; pouring out?
Chaubatik	—at the forked river; —a the river which abounds
Chibacoweda (Patience Island)	separated by a passage (from Prudence Island)
Chisawannock	—principal fishing place; —muddy bottom
Chockalaug	fox place
Conanicut (Jamestown)	at the especially long place (named after famous Narragansett Sachem Canonicus)
Conockonquit (Rose Island)	place at long point
Consumpsit	at the sharp rock
Coweset	place of young pine trees
Eschoheag, Escheague, Eastrig	—this is as far as the fish-spearing goes; —fork in the river where we spear fish ; —source of three rivers; —red land; a meadow
Hakewamepinke	end of the dry field or bank
Kickemuit	where the otter passes

5. See also under **Nations, Tribes, Villages**.

Mashanticut	small river or brook running through grove of trees
Massasoit	the great leader (Wampanoag)
Matunuck	high place or observation place
Maushapogue, Mashapaug, Maushapogue (Cranston)	land at the great cove
Miantonomi, Tonomy	he wages war (famous Narragansett Sachem)
Misquamicut	salmon place
Montup, Montaup, Montop	lookout place
Moosehousic, Mooshassuck, Mowshawsuck	at the great marsh
Moshasick, Moshassuck	great brook in the marshy meadow (part of Providence River; cf. Wanasquatucket)
Mosskituash	a place of reeds and rushes
Mouscochuck	a meadow
Nahiganset, Nahigonset	at the small point (cf. Narragansett. In historic times, called Nahicans)
Nannihiggonsick	—narrow strait; —good ferry
Nantusiunk (Goat Island)	narrow ford or stream
Narragansett	small narrow point
Nashaway	between two river branches
Nayatt	at the point
Neutaconanut, Natakonaket, Neotacacanonitt, Neutaqunkanet (Moondancer's favorite place to play and explore as a child)	at the short or scanty boundary point
Niantic	people of the point
Ninegrit	a war chief
Niswosaket (old name for Woonsocket)	water broken up as it goes rapidly downward?; place of two brooks
Nonequit	dry land
Occupessuatuxet, Occupasstuxet	small cove on the tidal river
Ohomowauke	place of owls
Pachaug	the turning place
Pascoag	the dividing place

Pawcomet (Beach Pond)	at the small beach
Pawtucket, Pattukket	at the water falls
Pesquamscot	at the cleft rock; split boulder place
Pocasset	where the stream widens
Pokanoket	at the clear land
Pometacomet	of the Massasoits' house?
Pomham, Pumham	he travels by sea (Narragansett Sachem & fierce warrior)
Ponaganset	—oyster processing place; —waiting place at the cove?
Pontiac (Ottawa language)	the falls in the river (after famous Indian Chief, Pontaic)
Popanomscutt	at the shelter (or roasting) rock
Poppasquash	—partridges; —broken rocks
Quawawehunk (place of Great Swamp Fight)	where the land shakes & trembles
Quonset	—long place; —round shallow cove
Sachuest	little hill at the outlet
Saconet, Sakonnet, Sagkonet	—black goose abode; —outlet
Scamscammuck	a red spring
Scituate	at the cold spring (or cold brook)
Shankhassick	at the hidden outlet of the stream
Shannock	where two streams meet
Shickasheen	good spring
Showamet (Warwick)	—at the peninsula, land between the waters; —at the neck (where we pull up our canoes)
Sowamsett	at the south country
Sowans	the south country
Touiset	at the great tidal riverusque
Wallomonopaug	—beautiful pond; —shallow pond; —dry pond?
Wallum	a dog?
Wanasquatucket	at the end of the tidal river (part of Providence River; cf. Moshassuck)
Wannemetonomy, Tonomy	good hills (lookout place)

Wappewassick (Prudence Island)	at the narrow straits
Watchaug	hill country
Waypoyset	at the narrows
Weekapaug	at the end of the pond
Woonsocket	—place of steep descent; —two brook place
Wyoming	large prairie (Delaware language)
Yawgoo	red pond?; fire place?; as far as this place?
Yawgoog	one side of the pond; here are many lice

OTHER NAMES

State of Connecticut

NAME[6]	TRANSLATION
Connecticut	place of long tidal river
Housatonic	beyond the mountain
Maanexit	path; gathering
Mashantucket	well-forested place
Mohegan	wolf people
Mystic	great tidal river
Naugatuck	one tree
Paucatuck, Pawcatuck	clear divided tidal stream
Pequot	destroyers
Quantisset	long brook
Quinebaug	long pond
Schaghticoke, Scaticook	where the river branches
Shantok	midway up the river
Sicaog (Hartford)	dark earth; muddy place
Wabquissit	west of the Quinebaug River

6. See also under **Nations, Tribes, Villages**.

APPENDIX III

Selected Quotes from Writings of Early American Colonists and Modern Indian Elders on Native American Women of Wampanoag, Narragansett & Massachusett Peoples

Their male children goe starke naked, and have no Apron untill they come to ten or twelve yeeres of age; their Female they, in a modest blush cover with a little Apron of an hand breadth from their very birth (Roger Williams, 1643).

The law which they observed in old times was this—to do to another only that which they wished to be done to them. ... All lived in good friendship & understanding. They refused no thing to one another. If one wigwam or family had not provisions enough, the neighbors supplied them, although they had only that which was necessary for themselves. And in all things it was the same. They lived pure lives; their wives were faithful to their husbands, and the girls were chaste (Nicholas Denys, 1672).

The older and married people, both men and women, wear many ornaments in their ears, hanging down in the oriental manner (*The Voyages of Giovanni da Verrazzano, 1524-1528*).

[.]... women and maids live apart in, foure, five, or six dayes, in the time of their monethly sicknesse, which custome in all parts of the Countrey they strictly observe, and no *Male* may come into that house (Roger Williams, 1643).

... Indian women ... are quickly and easily delivered and many times are so strong, not within a few hours after the child's birth, they will go about their ordinary occasions [back on their feet again] (Daniel Gookin, 1674).

They take many wives; yet one of them is the principal or chief in their esteem and affection. They also put away [divorce] their wives; and the wives also leave their husbands frequently, upon grounds of displeasure or dissatisfaction (Gookin, 1674).

Their infants are borne with hair on their heads and are of a complexion white as our nation [English], but their mothers in their infancy make a bath of Wallnut leaves, huskes of Walnuts [sic] and such things as will staine their skin for ever, wherein they dip and washe them to make them tawny (Thomas Morton, 1632).

Their women constantly beat all their corne with hand: they plant it, dresse it, gather it, barne it, beat it, and take as much paines as any people in the world, which labour is questionlesse one cause of their extraordinary ease of childbirth (Roger Williams, 1643).

It is almost incredible what burthens the poore women carry of *Corne*, of *Fish*, of *Beanes*, of *Mats*, and a childe besides (Roger Williams, 1643).

They likewise sew their husband's shoes and weave coats of feathers... (Wm. Wood, 1634).

Their Music is Lullabies

For their carriage it is very civil, smiles being their greatest grace of their mirth; their music is lullabies to quit their children, who generally are as quiet as if they had neither spleen or lungs. To hear one of these Indians unseen, a good ear might easily mistake their untaught voice for the warbling of a well-tuned instrument, such command have they of their voice (Wm. Wood, 1634).

The Tooth-ake

which is the only paine will force their stout hearts to cry; I cannot heare of any disease of the stone amongst them (the corne of the Countrey, with which they are fed from the wombe, being an admirable cleanser and opener) but the paine of their womens childbirth .... never forces their women to cry, as I have heard some of their men in this paine.

In this paine they use a certaine root dried, not much unlike our *Ginger* (Roger Williams, 1643).

When the Indian man hunted ages ago, they hunted for the whole village, leaving small children, women and the old ones at home (Oral tradition).

It may bee wondred why since *New-England* is about 12. degrees neerer to the Sun, yet some part of Winter it is there ordinarily more cold than here in *England*: the reason is plaine: All Ilands are warmer than maine Lands and Continents. *England* being an Iland, *Englands* winds are Sea winds, which are commonly more thick and vapoury, and warmer winds: The *Nor West* wind (occasioneth *New-England* cold) comes over the cold frozen Land, and over many millions of Loads of Snow: and yet the pure wholsomnesse of the Aire is wonderfull, and the warmth of the Sunne, such in the sharpest weather, that I have often seen the Natives Children runne about starke naked in the coldest dayes, and the *Indians,* Men and Women, lye by a Fire, in the Woods in the coldest nights, and I have been often out my selfe such nights without fire, mercifully, and wonderfully preserved (Roger Williams, 1643).

The Women set or plant, weede, and hill, and gather and barne all the corne, and Fruites of the field: Yet sometimes the man himselfe, (either out of love to his wife, or care for his Children, or being an old man) will help the Woman which (by the custome of the Countrey) they are not bound to.

When a field is to be broken up, they have a very loving sociable speedy way to dispatch it: All the neighbors men and Women forty, fifty, a hundred &c, joyne, and come in to help freely.

With friendly joyning they breake up their fields, build their Forts, hunt the Woods, stop and kill fish in the Rivers... (Roger Williams, 1643).

They have a two-fold nakednesse:

First ordinary and constant, when although they have a Beasts skin, or an English mantle on, yet that covers ordinarily but their hinder parts and all the foreparts from top to toe, (except their secret parts, covered with a little Apron ...) I say all else open and naked.

Their male children goe starke naked, and have no Apron untill they come to ten or twelve yeeres of age; their Female they, in a modest blush cover with a little Apron of an hand breadth from their very birth.

Their second nakedness is when their men often abroad, and both men and women within doores, leave off their beasts skin, or English cloth, and so (excepting their little Apron) are wholly naked; yet but few of the women but will keepe their skin or cloth (though loose) neare to them ready to gather it up about them.

Custome hath used their minds and bodies to it, and in such a freedom from any wantonnesse amongst them, as, (with griefe) I have heard of in *Europe* (Roger Williams, 1643).

As their apparel they wear breeches [leggings] and stockings in one, like some Irish; which is made of deer skins and have shoes [mocassins] of the same leather. They also wear a deer skin loose about them like a cloak which they will turn to the weather [wind] side.... The men wear also, when they go abroad in cold weather, an otter or fox skin on their right arm; but only their bracer [wristguard] on the left.

Women and all of that sex wear stings [of beads] about their legs which the men never do (Edward Winslow, 1624).

All their names are significant and variable for when they come to the state of men and women they alter them according to their deeds and dispositions (Winslow, 1624).

Besides there is a general custome amongst them, at the apprehension of any Excellency in Men, Women, Birds, Beast, Fish, &c. to cry out *Manittóo*, that is, it is a God, as thus if they see one man excell others in Wisdome, valour, strength, Activity &c. they cry out *Manittóo* A God: and therefore when they talk amongst themselves of the *English* ships, and great buildings, of the plowing of their Fields, and especially of Bookes and Letters, they will end thus: *Manittôwock* They are Gods: *Cummanittiôo*, you are a God, &c. A strong conviction naturall in the soule of man, that God is; filling all things, and places, and that all Excellencies dwell in God, and proceed from him ... (Roger Williams, 1643).

They believe that the soules of Men and Women goe to the Souwest, their great and good men and Women to *Cautàntouwit* his House, where they have hopes ... of carnall Joyes: Murthers thieves and Lyers, their Soules (say they) wander restlesse abroad (Roger Williams, 1643).

It hath pleased God in wonderfull manner to moderate that curse of sorrowes of Child-bearing to these poore Indian Women: So that ordinarily they have a wonderfull more speedy and easie Travell [pregnancy], and delivery then the Women of *Europe*: not that I thinke God is more gracious to them above other Women, but that it followes, First from the hardnesse of their constitution, in which respect they beare their sorrowes easier.

Secondly from their extraordinary great labour (even above the labour of men) as in the Field, they sustaine the labour of it, in carrying mighty Burthens, in digging clammes and getting other Shelfish from the Sea, in beating all their Corne in Morters &c.

Most of them count it a shame for a women in Travell to make complaint, and many of them scarcely heard to groane. I have often known in one Quarter of an houre a Woman merry in the House, and delevered and merry again: and within two dayes abroad, and foure or five dayes at worke &c. (Roger Williams, 1643).

There are among them certain men and women, whom they call powows ... partly are physicians, and make use ... of herbs and roots, for curing the sick and diseased (Daniel Gookin, 1674).

When a man hath a desire to marry, he first gets the good will of the maid or widow; after the consent of her friends for the part. As for himself, if he at his own disposing, if the king will, the match is made, the dowry of wampompeag paid, the king joins the hands with their hearts, never to part till death ... (Wm Wood, 1634).

They put away [divorce] frequently for other ocassions besides Adultery, yet I know many Couples that have lived twenty, thirty, fourty years together (Roger Williams, 1643).

The Love Signal was also chanted by young braves at this large festival [Harvest Festival, Moon of the Harvest] when so many young men and women met. When a young Indian girl became mature, her father gave a Festival of Pure Maidens every moon until she was chosen to be the mate of some young brave. At the ceremony a large white stone placed in the middle of the Council Fire was sprinkled with blood. The young girl was given an arrow which she placed over her heart with one hand and put the other hand on the stone while she took a vow of purity. Only the pure could participate in this Festival, so all the maidens were anxious to be virtuous so they qualify as the mate for some young brave. At the harvest festival many a pure Indian maiden received the song of love from the lips of an Indian youth (Princess Red Wing).

When the Lord first brought me to these poor Indians on the *Vinyard* they were mighty zealous and earnest in the Worship of false gods and Devils; their false gods were many, both of things in Heaven, Earth and Sea: And there they had their Men-gods, Women-gods, and Children-gods, their Companies, and Fellowships of gods, or Divine Powers, guiding things amongst men, innumerable more feigned gods belonging to many Creatures, to their Corn and every Colour of it: The Devil also with his Angels had his Kingdom among them, in them; account him they did the terror of Living, the god of the Dead, under whose cruel power and into whose deformed likeness they conceived themselves to be translated when they died; for the same word they have for *Devil*, they use for *a Dead Man*, in their Language (John Eliot & Thomas Mayhew, 1653).

Amongst themselves they trade their Corne, skins, Coates, Venison, Fish, &c. and sometimes come ten or twenty in a Company to trade amongst the *English.*

They have some who follow onely making of Bowes, some Arrowes, some Dishes, and (the Women make all their earthen Vessells) some follow fishing, some hunting: most on the Sea-side make [wampum], and store up shells in Summer against Winter whereof to make their [wampum] (Roger Williams, 1643).

Keesaqúnnamun, Another kind of solemne publike meeting, wherein they lie under the trees, in a kinde of Religious observation, and have a mixture of Devotions and sports: But their chiefest Idoll of all for sport and game, is (if their land be at peace) toward Harvest, when they set up a long house called *Qunnèkamuck.* Which signifies *Longhouse*, sometimes an hundred, sometimes two hundred foot long upon a plaine neer the Court (which they call *Kitteickaúick*) where many thousands, men and women meet, where he that goes in danceth in the sight of all the rest; and is prepared for money, coats, small breeches, knifes, or what hee is able to reach to, and gives these things away to the poore, who yest must particularly beg and say, *Cowequetúmmous,* that is, I *beseech you;* which word (although there is not one common beggar amongst them) yet they will often use when their richest amongst them would fain obtain ought by gift (Roger Williams, 1643).

That is, he hath some dead in his house (whether wife or child &c.) for although at the first being sicke, all the Women and Maides blacke their faces with soote and other blackings; yet upon the death of the sicke, the father, or husband, and all his neighbors, the men also ... weare blacke *Faces*, and lay on soote very thicke, which I have often seene clotted with their tears.

This blacking and lamenting they observe in mist dolefull manner, divers weekes and monthes; yea, a yeere. if the person be great and publike (Roger Williams, 1643).

The Indian woman were getting ready for their Strawberry Thanksgiving over in Plymouth and hung their babies on the trees all around the fields while they were picking wild strawberries for their feast. Then they put one young Indian to watch.

And while he was watching, he began singing a song and whittling a stick. By and by a Pilgrim man sat down beside him. The Indian, he kept right on singing, kept right on whittling. By and by the Pilgrim man nudged him and said, "I like your song, I like your song" as he pointed to his lips. By and by the Indian understood what he was talking about and said, "Wind rock baby, but by and by wind blow fast, bough break, down come babies' cradle and all." And he laughed when he thought what a squall it would be if they all came tumbling down at once (traditional; recorded in Princess Red Wing, 1986).

If it be the man or woman of the house, they will pull down the mats, and leave the frame standing, and bury them in or near the same, and either remove their dwelling or give over house-keeping (from Winslow).

As they abound in lamentations for the dead, so they abound in consolation to the living, and visit them frequently, using this word *Kutchímmoke, Kutchímmoke,* Be of good cheere, which they expresse by stroaking the cheeke and head of the father or mother, husband, or wife of the dead (Roger Williams, 1643).

The women in the times of their mourning, after the death of their husbands or kindred, do paint their faces all over black, like a negro; and so continue in this posture many days (Daniel Gookin, 1674).

APPENDIX IV

Selection of Some Europeans Who Wrote About New England Indians in the 1500s, 1600s, 1700s

Source: *Newsletter of Aquidneck Indian Council, Vol. 3*

European Writer's Name and Dates	Location He Describes	Indian Tribal People Described in Southern New England
Early Explorers of 1600's— Bartholemew Gosnold, Martin Pring, George Waymouth, Henry Hudson, John Smith, Thomas Dermer, Marc Lescobot & others	New England Coast	Various Algonquian-speaking tribal groups
Giovanni da Verrazzano (writing 1524-1650)	Narragansett Bay	Wampanoag (Pokanokets) or maybe Narragansetts

Samuel De Champlain (map, 1600)	New England Coast	Wampanoag (Pokanokets) & others
Adrian Block (writing 1614)	Narragansett Bay	Wampanoag (Pokanokets) or maybe Narragansetts
Edward Winslow (1595-1655)	Plymouth Colony	Wampanoag (Pokanokets) & Narragansetts & Massachusetts
William Bradford (1590-?)	Plymouth Colony	Wampanoag (Pokanokets) & Narragansetts & Massachusetts
William Wood (writing 1634)	Northern Mass. Bay & Naumkeag area	Pawtuckets & Nipmucks & Massachusetts & Western Abenaki [? not sure] (Wood wrote 1st Indian vocabulary]
Thomas Morton (writing 1637)	Qunicy, Mass.	Massachusetts
Roger Williams (1603?-1683)	Rhode Island	Narragansetts [Language book]
John Josselyn (writing 1672-1674)	New England Coast	Eastern Abenakis (Maine)
John Winthrop, Sr. (writing 1630-1649)	Mass. Bay Colony	Massachusetts & Narragansetts & Pequots
John Winthrop, Jr. (? who knows—write us)	lower/middle Connecticut River Valley	Pequots & Western Abenakis (? not sure)
John Eliot (1604-1690)	Mass. Bay Colony [Lang. expert]	Massachusetts and Nipmucks
Daniel Gookin (1612-1687)	Mass. Bay Colony	All tribes in region
Thomas Mayhew, Jr. (1621-1657)	Martha's Vineyard [Lang. expert]	Wampanoag (Pokanokets)
Thomas Mayhew, Sr. (died 1682)	Martha's Vineyard [Lang. expert]	Wampanoag (Pokanokets)
Mathew Mayhew (died 1710)	Martha's Vineyard [Lang. expert]	Wampanoag (Pokanokets)
John and Josiah Cotton (writing 1707)	Plymoth Colony [Lang. expert]	Wampanoag (Pokanokets)
William Pynchons (born 1589 ?)	Connecticut River Valley	Pocumtucks
John Pynchons (writing 1642-1670)	Connecticut River Valley	Pocumtucks

Other Sources for Colonial Writings & References

Massachusetts State Archives, 220 Morrisey Blvd., Boston, MA 02125, open Mon-Fri. 9-5, Sat 9-3. Tel ~ 1-617-727-2816 [colonial period documents of 1600s, 1700s, 1800s, on microfilm].

INTERNET<>http://www.geocities.com/Athens/Oracle/7595/wamp1.htm.

Trigger, Bruce G. (Volume Editor, 1978). *Handbook of North American Indians*, vol. 15 (*Northeast*). Washington, DC: Smithsonian Institution [standard scholarly book].

Lenz, Peter A. (1995a). *Skicinuwok Wanbanaghi or People of the Aurora*, 1621-1625, vol. 2, Part 1. Norway, ME: Maine Performing Arts and Humanities, Inc. [Lenz has many good maps, long excerpts and help with Colonial-style English].

Lenz, Peter A. (1995b). *Skicinuwok Wanbanaghi or People of the Aurora*, 1621-1625, vol. 2, Part 2. Norway, ME: Maine Performing Arts and Humanities, Inc. [Lenz has many good maps, long excerpts and help with Colonial-style English].

Lenz, Peter A. (1995c). *Skicinuwok Wanbanaghi or People of the Aurora*, 1621-1625, vol. 2, Part 3. Norway, ME: Maine Performing Arts and Humanities, Inc. [Lenz has many good maps, long excerpts and help with Colonial-style English].

We recommend the Lenz books (abstracts of the old works with commentary). Receive a listing of his other available publications on Algonquians and also Black-Slavery & Jewish Holocaust. Write to: P. Lenz, RR2, Box 1020. Norway, ME 04268 for catalogue.

APPENDIX V

Bringing Back Our Lost Language

A paper presented at Carpenter Museum before The Rehoboth Antiquarian Society and The Annawan Historical Society, Rehoboth, MA, March 11, 1998.

Introduction

Before the Europeans came to these shores in search of wealth and religious freedom for themselves, about 12,000 Wampanoag Indians lived here in southeastern New England—about 8,000 on the mainland and about 4,000 on the islands. After the King Philip's War (1675-1676) only about 400 Wampanoag people survived. No one has done a complete history of all these people following the war.

Over the years the forces of blood mixing, enactment of laws, disease, racial attitude, and isolation have disintegrated the looks, language and lore of the First Americans of our region. But Indian culture was never completely replaced by Christianity or European culture. A people does not want to die!

The ancient language of the Wampanoag Indians, and related Algonquian-speakers, is called nowadays *Massachusett*. This language, like most Indian languages, was oral. It was the language spoken by the Massasoit Ousa Mequin, and by Annawan, and all of the Indians that lived in this region.

The Massachusett language has been sleeping since the early 1800s. Even in the early 1700s, some were not speaking fluently the language anymore. Because our ancestors were considered a conquered people and no longer able to practice our culture, the new ways of Europeans slowly replaced many of the old ways. It seems that the parents and grandparents just refused to teach their children the old language, maybe because they saw the pain involved in being Indian in a world no longer theirs.

Eventually the old language fell silent, as did all of the Indian languages across southern New England, from Cape Cod and beyond to the Hudson River. Across Turtle Island—what we call the United States of America—over 125 American Indian languages have become extinct through the harsh lessons of American history. Many more are on the brink of extinction.

Today many people want their ancient Massachusett language back and are willing to work hard to learn a very complicated language. A language is the essence of one as a human being. Knowing the language of ones Native American ancestors makes one unmistakably Indian. Rebuilding the Massachusett language involves intense research and cooperation among Indians, language scholars and others. Next to no funding is available to tribes or Councils who want to bring back their lost language.

The Massachusett Language

Let's give a brief overview of how the oral language was recorded. In 1620 when the English landed at Plymouth, MA they walked into the abandoned village of Patuxet. The English were on the land of the Wampanoag. When a separate group of English landed in 1630 [first in Salem, MA, then Boston, MA] they entered the land of the Massachusêuck (The Massachuset People or "People of the Great Hills"). The Massachusêuck, the Wampanoag and other indigenous people along the coast, were victims of catastrophic diseases introduced by previous European explorers as early as 1612-1613. The mortality rate reached 90%. This is the main reason why Europeans met virtually no resistance when they came ashore.

Up in the Boston area, the charter of the Massachusetts Bay Company said that the principal aim of the English colony was to "incite" the Native peoples to accept and practice the Christian religion. Certain laws were even passed later to insure that the Indians would accept Christianity and not practice their own religion.

Only the English missionaries took seriously this goal of conversion. One English name stands out above all others in connection with the recording of the language of the Wampanoag and other Algonquian-speaking peoples of southeastern New England. This man was John Eliot, a Congregationalist Minister who came to New England in 1631. Eliot began to learn this unwritten language. He was convinced that only by being able to communicate with native peoples in their own language could he achieve the goal of spreading Christianity to the Indians. One day the local Massachusett Sachem called Waban asked Eliot to explain Christian teachings. Later Eliot and his now "praying Indians" founded a European-styled village at Natick, MA. This village was called a "praying village". Here Eliot worked with his devoted teacher (and servant of 35 years) Job Nesutan to learn the language. Eliot worked with Job Nesutan and other Indians in translating the Holy Bible into the Massachusett language. The Indian Bible (written entirely in the local Natick dialect of Massachusett) was published in 1663 at Harvard University and a second edition was printed in 1685 (so many Bibles were destroyed in the King Philip's War, 1675-1676).

Other Indians that made possible the translation and publication of the Bible are John Sassamon, Cochenoe and James Printer. Hardly anyone ever mentions the necessary contributions of the Indians. Without these Indians there would have been no Bible. If Issac Newton, one of the greatest European scientists could humbly claim he stood on the shoulders of giants to accomplish his work, we can say the same of John Eliot and his Indian teachers.

Now, the Indian Bible is not the way Indians spoke the Massachusett language. Like the English language Bible with its abstract language, the Indian Bible was meant to teach the Christian faith which is very different from the Indian religion. But the Eliot Bible is one of the most important primary sources we have for the pronunciation, vocabulary and grammar of the language. In fact, the Massachusett language is perhaps the only language which has any chance of being revived since we know more about this language than any other in the region.

It is ironic that the missionary John Eliot, who came here to destroy Indian culture, actually preserved the language in written form. We must be thankful to the Natick Indian Job Nesutan, and John Sassamon, Cochenoe and James Printer for they ultimately are the safekeepers of our language.

Narragansett Language

The Narragansett language, once spoken by the Narragansetts, is quite similar to Massachusett. Narragansett was understood throughout New England. Scholars refer to Massachusett and Narragansett as dialects of the same language. Narragansett was partially recorded by Roger Williams and published in his book *A Key into the Language of America* in 1643. Williams was writing a book so that the English who came here would have a phrase book to use in communicating with the local people. This book is well worth getting. His book seems to give some of the actual speech patterns of the Narragansetts (and the Wampanoag). Williams did a better job than Eliot of recording the sounds of the language.

The Massachusett Language as Written by Indians

Ten years ago a book came out called *Native Writings in Massachusett* by Ives Goddard and Kathleen Bragdon, two of the top scholars who work on the technical aspects of our language. This book is actually in two volumes. The first volume has writings from Wampanoag Indians of the 1600s and 1700s. The second volume is very technical, dealing with grammar of the language.

Teaching the Language

Last year we published the first book written for Indians on the language. The textbook—*Understanding Algonquian Indian Words (New England)*—was published with the help of a grant from the Rhode Island Committee for the Humanities (a state program of the National Endowment for the Humanities). We give about 1,400 entries in the dictionary part of the book and cover grammar and other aspects of the language at a very basic level for the beginning learner[†].

We are recognized throughout the area as knowledgeable about the language. Several years ago the Rhode Island Committee for the Humanities contacted us to provide a Massachusett language translation to be carved on a permanent monument in Providence, RI. This engraving may be one of the few public testaments of the Indian tongues spoken here for over 12,000 years.

Since the time of our book's publication, our Council has been preparing many classroom teaching materials on the language. Our efforts at reviving the language involve making up teaching materials to instruct tribal members on pronunciation, vocabulary and grammar. These materials along with the book can allow us to teach the elements of the Massachusett-Narragansett language. A second language book—*A Massachusett Language Book, Vol. 1*— was the result of our recent efforts to bring the language back to our brothers and sisters here in southeastern New England.

The following diagram shows the main sources we use in our research into the language. The references are given at the back of this book.

[†]We acknowledge the assistance of our Principal Humanities Scholars, Tall Oak (Council Elder), and Karl V. Teeter (Professor Emeritus of Linguistics, Harvard University). We also acknowledge the guidance, support and love of the late Slow Turtle, Supreme Medicine Man of the Wampanoag Nation.

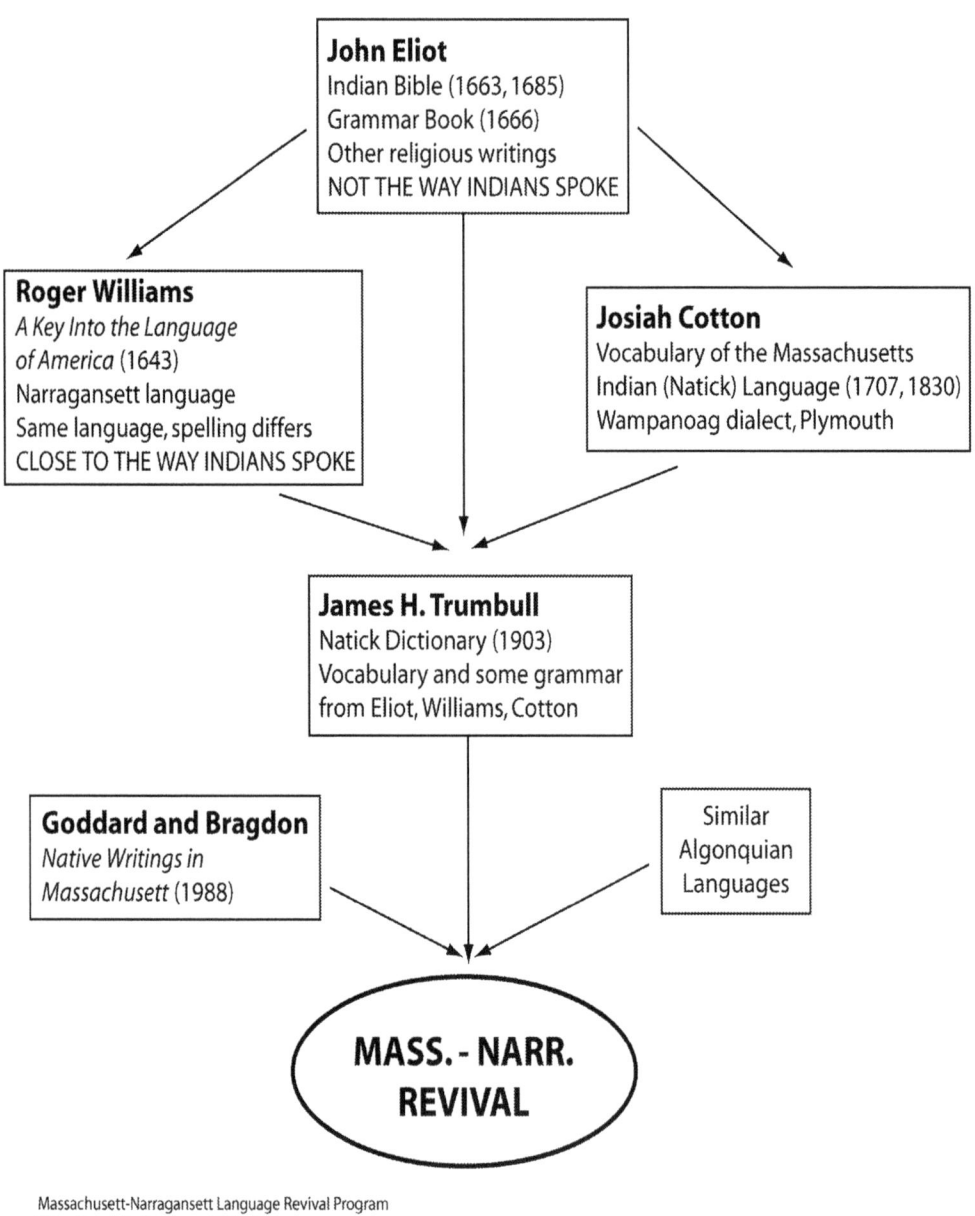

Figure 4. Sources of Information for the Massachusett Language Revival Program. Sources given in References at back of book.

APPENDIX VI
PRONUNCIATION GUIDE

Guide to Historic Spellings & Sounds in *Massachusett-Narragansett*

(Mainland Dialects from Records of 1600s & 1700s)

STRESS AND PITCH MARKS

STRESS (Accent)   *LANGUAGE*
á (primary or main stress)   Massachusett & Narragansett
à (secondary stress)   Historic records seem to omit

PITCH (Tone)	LANGUAGE
á (high or rising)	Narragansett?
à (low or falling)	Narragansett?
â (rising, then falling)	Narragansett [in Massachusett ^ symbol is for nasals— â, ô, û]
m' (pause, hesitation)	Massachusett & Narragansett

SYLLABLE STRESS

Stress (or emphasis or accent) typically falls on syllable or syllables marked with special symbols (e.g., wétu stresses first syllable with primary/main stress; ewò stresses second with a low/falling tone; wuskówhàn has main stress & low pitch; aúï stresses aú *and* ï).

Narragansett is well-stressed, although inconsistently and ambiguously (G. Aubin, 1972). Most Massachusett language words in Eliot seem to have no stress marks. This may indicate either that no special stress on any one syllable exists [e.g., nippe, ask∞k, mehtugq], or it was omitted intentionally for fluent speakers of the language being taught the Bible in their own oral language.

Algonquianist Professor G. Aubin, a respected correspondent of the Aquidneck Indian Council, relates in a personal e-mail communication of 6-25-2002, the possible applicability of the following efficient "Ojibway-like rule" for long/short vowels shown below (cf. Goddard and Bragdon, 1988):

* All long vowels are stressed
* All alternate even-numbered short vowels are stressed

This rule presupposes the existence of correct vowel classification which has not been achieved for the extinct American Indian languages Massachusett-Narragansett. Consequently, accent and "pronunciation" in this extinct American Indian language group is largely intuitive; it is also based significantly on imitating the sounds from "similar" existing Algonquian languages such as Maliseet/Passamaquoddy which are documented in the theoretical and educational literature.

VOWELS & CONSONANTS (true "phonemes"). See the list below for other vowel spellings & sounds.

Six Vowels
- u   short
- a   short
- ee   long
- o   long
- oo   long
- ô   long

Twelve Consonants
ch, h, k, m, n, p, s, sh, t, tt, te, t^y, w, y

Partial List of Spellings & Sounds

SPELLING (from John Eliot & others)	APPROXIMATE SOUND (Some are uncertain)
a [as in wadchu ("wachuw")]	a in sofa (or) ah [short or long version]
aa [as in waantam∞onk]	long ah [sometimes aa written as aá]
á [as in násh ("nosh")]	long ah
ā [as in wâwāmek]	a in ale (or) a in father
ă [as in pă]	a in abet
â [as in nâmaus]	a in French word blanc (â is a nasal sound) (or, perhaps) ah [long vesion]
å̂	a in knave (nasalized). is rarely seen
ä [as in peäsik]	a in arm (rarely seen)
ae [word middle or ending]	e in he (or) a in am
áe [word middle or ending as in agkomáe ("akomôee")]	ah-ee (long ah)
ag [as in tannag ("tanok")]	ak as in clock
ah [word ending]	long ah
ai [as in naish ("nosh")]	long ah (or) ai in mail
aih [as in nuppaih ("nupoh")]	ah [long version]
am, an, ám, án [after consonant as in sampwe ("sôpwee")]	a in French blanc (nasal sound)

ash [word ending for plurals as in hassenash]	arsh in harsh (silent r)
ass [word ending for some plurals, Narragansett]	ahs
au [as in hennau ("henôw")]	ow
aû [as in aûke ("ahkee"), Narr.]	long ah [a rising-falling pitch]
aú, áu [as in nesáusuk ("neesôsuk")]	nasal sound ô as a in French blanc
aü [as in aü]	ah-ou (ü is oo in boot)
b, bp [word middle after vowel as in kobhog ("kophak")]	b or p in big (or) pig (a sound between b / p)
b, bp [word ending]	b or p in big (or) pig (a sound between b / p)
ca, co, cu	k-sound like call, cold, cut
cau	cow (or) caw (see kau)
ce, ci	s-sound in cede, civil, acid; sometimes z- or sh-sound as in sacrifice, ocean
ch [word beginning and after h]	ch in chair
ch [word middle & word ending after vowel]	chh, etching
cha [word beginning]	cha in cha-cha
cha, che, chi [word middle & ending, as in sâchem ("sôteum")]	tee-you [fast tempo] (a complex sound between ch & t)
che, chee	chee in cheese
chu [word middle following vowel or word ending as in wechu ("wee-teuw")]	tee-you [fast tempo] (a complex sound between ch & t). chu is rarely seen with this sound as a word ending; see next entry for more common sound with this word ending.
chu [word ending as in wadchu; ("wachuw") & meechu; ("meechuw")]	chew
ckq [word middle as in Narr., muck-quétu ("mukweeteuw")]	qu as in queen (see kq)
dch, dtch [word middle & word ending after vowel]	ch in much, etching
dj	ch in match (rare)

dt, d [word middle after vowel]	t in tin (or) d in din (a d-t sound) [d may be silent in some words like wad-chu ("wachuw")]
dt, d [word ending as in kod ("kat")]	t in tin (or) d in din (a d-t sound)
dtea [after a vowel]	tee-ah [fast tempo] (a complex sound between ch & t)
dti	tee-you [fast tempo] (a complex sound between ch & t)
e [word beginning or middle as in kesukun ("keesukun")]	e in he (or) a in sofa (or) e in bed (Narr.)
e [word ending as in wuske ("wus kee") or seipe ("seep")]	e in he [usually for adjectives & adverbs; a final e in some Roger Williams & Cotton words is probably silent and tells us that the preceeding vowel is a long sound; e.g. cummú-muckquete ("kumumukweet") (see ese for another example)
ē	e in he
ee	ee as in green (or, before ht & hch) a in sofa
é [as in wétu ("weeteuw")]	e in he
ĕ [as in mĕtah]	e in end
ê [Narr., as in pennêtunck ("pehnêtunck")]	Roger Williams says ^ is "long sounding Accent"
ë	a in tame (ë rarely seen)
ea [as in sekeneam ("seekuniam")]	e in he (or) long ah
ei [as in keihtoh ("kuhtah")]	a in sofa [before ht, hch] (or) i in hit (or, rarely) ee in heed
emes [word ending for diminutive as in mehtugquemes ("muhtuk weemees")]	eemees
es [word ending for diminutive as in mehtugques ("muhtukwees")]	ees
ese [word ending for Narr. diminutive, as in squáese ("skwahees")]	ees [final e in ese probably silent & means preceeding vowel is "long"; see e (word ending)]
et [word ending, "locative" as in pau-tuxet]	et in set

eu [as in a<u>yeu</u> ("ayuw")]	<u>eu</u> in feud
êuck [word ending as in Narr., Massachus<u>êuck</u>]	<u>e</u> in heed + <u>ook</u> in hook
f	not used
g, gg, gk [word middle after a vowel as in a<u>gk</u>omáe ("akomôee")]	<u>k</u> in cow [perhaps a guttural sound]; one g heard in gg.
g, gk [word ending as in mehtu<u>g</u> ("muhtukw") & tan<u>n</u>a<u>g</u> ("tanok")]	<u>k</u> in cow [perhaps a guttural sound] (or) <u>qu</u> in queen
gh	<u>k</u> in cow (or) <u>ge</u> in age
ghk	<u>k</u> in cow (or) <u>qu</u> in queen
gi, ji	<u>gi</u> in giant
gq [word ending as in mehtu<u>gq</u> ("muhtukw")]	<u>qu</u> in queen
gw, gqu [word middle between vowels as in mehtu<u>gqu</u>ash ("muhtukwash")]	<u>qu</u> in queen
h, hh	<u>h</u> in hot (one <u>h</u> heard)
h' [word beginning as in <u>h'</u>tugk]	<u>h</u> in hot (a pause or breathing sound after <u>h</u>)
hch, ch	<u>ch</u> in chair
hk [word middle as in ki<u>shk</u>e ("keeskee")]	<u>k</u> in cow
hsh	<u>sh</u> in shoe
ht	<u>ht</u> in height
hw, hwh	<u>wh</u> in what
i [word middle as in qu<u>i</u>nni ("kwinee")]	<u>a</u> in sofa (or) <u>e</u> in he (or) <u>i</u> in hit (Narr.)
i [word ending as in m∞<u>i</u> ("moowee")]	<u>e</u> in he
í [as in s<u>i</u>ckíssuog]	<u>i</u> in hit (or) <u>a</u> in sofa (or) <u>i</u> in hit (Narr.)
ī	<u>i</u> in ice
ĭ [as in nehch<u>ĭ</u>ppog]	<u>i</u> in ill
ï [as in aúï]	<u>e</u> in he (ï rarely seen)
ie	<u>e</u> in he [rare]
is, ish [word middle as in ki<u>sh</u>ke ("keeskee")]	<u>ees</u> [see entry for sh & shk]
ish [word ending as in an<u>ish</u> ("ahnish")]	<u>ish</u> as in dish

is [word ending as in mokkis ("mahkus")]	us
it, ut [word ending, "locative"]	it or ut in put
j	ch in match (or) gi in giant (rare)
ji	gi in giant
jt [word middle after vowel as in qua-jtog ("kwochtak")]	ch in etching
k [word beginning & after consonant]	k in cow
k, kk [word middle after vowel as in mokkis ("mahkus")]	k in cow (one k heard)
k [word ending as in ahtuk ("ahtukw")]	qu in queen (or) k in cow
k' [word beginning as in k'chi]	2nd k in kick (a pause or breathing sound after k)
kau	cow (or) caw (see cau)
ke	kee in keep (or) kuh
kē, kee	kee in keep
kh	ck in back?
ki	kee in keep (or) ki in kick
ko	ka in karate (or) co in coop
kq [before consonant & word ending]	qu in queen [see ckq]
kqu [word middle between vowels as in nukqutchtamup ("nukwuch tamup")]	qu in queen [see ckq]
kuh, keh [as in keht∞nog ("kuhtoonakw")]	uh like a in sofa (or) kuh in coop
l	el (rarely seen in southeastern New England dialects)
m, mm	m in mud (or) hammer (one m heard)
ṁ [as in ("pôhpuw")]	nasal sound as in pomp (is very rare)
m' [word beginning as in m'tugk]	meh or muh (a pause or breathing sound after m)
n [beginning of word]	n in no
nn [beginning of word as in nnin]	ne-ne in enema (two n sounds)
n, nn [middle, end of word]	ne-ne in enema (two n sounds)
ṅ [as in moṅchu]	oṅ is nasal sound

o [as in k<u>o</u>d ("kat")]	<u>ah</u> [short version] (or) <u>oo</u> in food
oo [as in <u>a</u>skook]	<u>oo</u> in food
oooo, ∞	first oo or ∞ spoken; said as <u>oo</u> in food
ó [as in w<u>ó</u>mpi ("wampee") & an<u>ó</u>me ("anôme")]	<u>ah</u> [long version] (or, rarely) <u>o</u> in old
ō [as in k<u>ō</u>muk]	<u>o</u> in old
ô [as in w<u>ô</u>skétomp ("waskeetôp")]	<u>a</u> in French word blanc (nasal sound)
ô̂	<u>o</u> in no [as a nasal sound?] is very rare.
ock [word middle or ending, Narr.]	<u>ak</u> in clock
og [word middle or ending]	<u>ak</u> in clock
oh [as in <u>oh</u>ke ("ahkee")]	<u>ah</u> [short or long version] (or) nasal sound ôh [after <u>n</u>]
ōh [as in p<u>ō</u>hqui]	<u>a</u> in sofa
oi	<u>oi</u> in oil
ôi	nasal <u>a</u> in blanc + <u>e</u> in he
om, on [nasal sound as in w<u>ô</u>skétomp("waskeetôp")]	<u>a</u> in French word blanc (nasal sound)
onk [word ending, abstract nouns as in meets<u>uonk</u>]	<u>onck</u> (or) <u>unck</u>
oo [as in <u>a</u>skook ("ahskook")]	<u>oo</u> in food [Eliot's special symbol for double oo; the same as ∞ (or) 8]
∞ [as in m<u>utt∞</u>n ("mutoon")]	<u>oo</u> in food (modern symbol for oo; 8 also used for ∞)
∞, ∞∞	first o or ∞ spoken; said as <u>oo</u> in food
∞̄ [as in sohsum<u>∞̄</u>nk]	<u>oo</u> in boot
∞̆ [as in peatam<u>∞̆</u>onk]	<u>oo</u> in foot
ou	<u>ou</u> in out
∞w [word beginning]	wh<u>ee</u> ("whistling sound" which Eliot couldn't explain]
p, pp [word middle after vowel]	<u>p</u> or <u>b</u> in pig (or) big (a sound between <u>p</u> / <u>b</u>). One <u>p</u> heard
p [word ending]	<u>p</u> or <u>b</u> in pig (or) big (a sound between <u>p</u> / <u>b</u>)
ps [word beginning or middle as in <u>p</u>suk]	<u>pss</u> (rare)
pu, puh [as in a<u>pu</u> ("apuw")]	<u>pu</u> in put
q [before consonant & word ending]	<u>qu</u> in queen

qu [word beginning & after consonant]	qu in queen
qu [word middle between vowels]	qu in queen
qua [as in quadjtog ("kwochtak")]	quo in quota (or) qua in quality
quâ	quo in Pequot
que [as in ahque ("ahkwee")]	quee in queen (or) quest
qui	quee in queen (or) qui in quick
quie [as in wishquie ("weeskwayee")]	kwayee
quo [as in ahquompi ("ahkwahmpee")]	quah
qun [as in qunutug ("kwunutukw")]	kwun
qū [as in qutshau]	coo (like dove-sound)
qut	kwut
r	are (rarely used in southeastern New England dialects)
s [word beginning & after consonant]	s in sip
s, ss [after vowel as in nusseet ("nuseet")]	s in sip (one s sound)
sh [before vowel & word ending as in mukquoshim ("mukwahshum")]	sh in shoe, she, ship
sh [before consonant as in kishke ("keeskee")]	s in sip
shau [as in petshau ("peetshow")]	show in rain-shower
shk [before vowel as in kishke ("keeskee")]	sk in Alaska
sq [as in mosq ("mahskw")]	squah in squat
suck [word ending, for plurals in Narragansett]	sook
t [word beginning & after consonant as in taûbot]	t in tin (or) d in din (a d-t sound)
t, tt [word middle after vowel as in nuttah ("nutah")]	t in tin (or) d in din (a d-t sound) [one t heard]
t, tt [word end as in moskeht]	tee-you [fast tempo] (a complex sound between ch & t)
tch [word middle & word ending after vowel]	ch in etching
te [word beginning as in teag ("teokw")]	tee-you [fast tempo] (a complex sound between ch & t))

201

tea, ttea [after a vowel]	tee-ah [fast tempo] (a complex sound between ch & t)
teau, teu, tteu [word middle or end as in keteau ("keeteow")]	tee-you [fast tempo] (a complex sound between ch & t)
to, tó, tô [as in attóau ("atôow")]	to in top [a nasal sound]
tu, ttu [word middle or end as in wétu ("weeteuw"), pittu (puteow")]	tee-you [fast tempo] (a complex sound between ch & t); Other sounds like ti, tti, tj have the tee-you sound plus additional sounds
toh [as in kehtoh ("kuhtah")]	tah
u [as in wuttup ("wutup")]	a in sofa (or) ah (short version). Some think that at the beginning of some words, a u was a "whistling sound" (see w)
ú [as in aúi]	u in rude (or) a in sofa
ū [as in qūtshaü]	u in rude, tune
ŭ [as in wonkqŭssis]	u in circus, up?
û	a in blanc (or) u in mud? (nasal sound)
u̇	u in turner (in Eliot?)
ü [as in aü]	u in upsilon (or) oo in boot (ü rarely seen)?
uck, uk [word ending as in pasuk ("posukw")]	k is qu sound as in queen
ut, it [word ending, "locative" as in kehtompskut]	ut in put (or) it
uw [word beginning]	a w "whistling sound"
v	not used
w, ww	w in won (one w heard) [perhaps a "whistling sound" in some words beginning with w]
wh	wh in what
wi	why (or) wee
wu [as in wuttup ("wutup")]	wah (or) woo
x	ex in exit (rarely seen)
y	y in yes
ȳ	y in lyre (in Eliot, others?)
ỹ	y in typical (or) fully

yau	yaw
yeu [as in ayeu ("ayuw")]	you
yo	yah (or) yo in yo-yo
yó	yah (or) yo in yo-yo
yō	yo in yo-yo
z, zs [as in nukkezheomp ("nukeeshiôp")]	s in sip

NOTE: The above spellings are selected from the works of John Eliot, Josiah Cotton, Roger Williams & J. H. Trumbull. The Nantucket & Martha's Vineyard "island dialects" are not included. The symbols ∞ and 8 are seen in modern writings to stand for Eliot's special character oo. There is a great deal of uncertainty in our knowledge about the actual speech sounds and patterns of the Algonquian-speaking full-blooded Indians of southeastern New England (Rhode Island, Massachusetts & parts of Connecticut). For additional information on these matters of phonology, consult the works by Goddard (1981), Goddard & Bragdon (1988), and others.

APPENDIX VII

THE WHITE HOUSE

Office of the Press Secretary
(Cape Canaveral, Florida)
For Immediate Release
October 29, 1998

NATIONAL AMERICAN INDIAN HERITAGE MONTH, 1998

- - - - - - -

BY THE PRESIDENT OF THE UNITED STATES OF AMERICA

A PROCLAMATION

American Indians and Alaska Natives—the first Americans—have made enormous contributions to the life of our country. When the first Europeans arrived on this continent, they did not find an empty land; they found instead a land of diverse peoples with a rich and complex system of governments, languages, religions, values, and traditions that have shaped and influenced American history and heritage. Generations of American Indians have served and sacrificed to defend our freedom, and no segment of our population has sent a larger percentage of its young men and women to serve in our Armed Forces. But American Indians are not just an important part of our country's past; they are also a vital part of today's America and will play an even more important role in America's future.

There are more than 2 million American Indians living in our country today, from the hardwood forests of Maine to the Florida Everglades, across the Great Plains to the Pacific Coast, and throughout the State of Alaska. Through a variety of innovative enterprises, many tribes are sharing in the unprecedented prosperity our country enjoys today, prosperity that is reflected in the construction of community centers, schools, museums, and other cultural centers. However, many people who live in Indian Country are caught in a cycle of poverty made worse by poor health care and a lack of educational and employment opportunity. If we are to honor the United States Government's long-standing obligations to Indian tribes, we must do all in our power to ensure that American Indians have access to the tools and opportunities they need to make the most of their lives.

As part of this endeavor, my Administration has strengthened the special government-to-government relationship between the Federal Government and the sovereign nations of Indian Country, expanded the role of American Indians and Alaska Natives in the Administration, and sought to increase educational opportunities and economic development throughout Indian Country. Earlier this year, I signed an Executive order directing the Federal Government to work together with tribal and State governments to improve Native American achievement in math and reading, raise high school graduation rates, increase the number of Native American youth attending college, improve science education, and expand the use of educational technology. We are also striving to boost economic development in Indian Country by working with tribal governments to meet their technology infrastructure needs, to coordinate and strengthen existing Native American economic development initiatives, and to help Native Americans obtain loans more easily for building homes and starting new businesses. Today's Native Americans are among the youngest segments of our population—a new, large generation of young people who, if empowered with the education, skills, opportunity, and encouragement they need to thrive, can lead Indian Country into a future as bright and promising as its extraordinary past. As we observe National American Indian Heritage Month, let us resolve to work together to make that future a reality.

NOW, THEREFORE, I, WILLIAM J. CLINTON, President of the United States of America, by virtue of the authority vested in me by the Constitution and laws of the United States, do hereby proclaim November 1998 as National American Indian Heritage Month. I urge all Americans, as well as their elected representatives at the Federal, State, local, and tribal levels, to observe this month with appropriate programs, ceremonies, and activities.

IN WITNESS WHEREOF, I have hereunto set my hand this twenty-ninth day of October, in the year of our Lord nineteen hundred and ninety-eight, and of the Independence of the United States of America the two hundred and twenty-third.

WILLIAM J. CLINTON

REFERENCES & SOURCES

[see Appendix IV for other sources]

Aquidneck Indian Council Newsletter. Newport, RI: Aquidneck Indian Council, Inc.

Attaquin, Helen A.A. (1970) *A Brief History of Gay Head or Aquinnah.* (self-published).

Aubin, George (1972). *A Historical Phonology of Narragansett.* Providence, RI: Ph.D. Dissertation, Brown University.

Baraga, Frederic (1878, 1992). *A Dictionary of the Ojibway Language.* St. Paul, MN: Minnesota Historical Society.

Benjamin, Mary (1999, forthcoming). *The Memoirs of Princess Red Wing.*

Bicknell, Thomas W. (1908). *Sowams.* New Haven, CT: Associated Publishers of American Records.

Bonfanti, Leo (1993). *Biographies and Legends of the New England Indians*, Vol. 1. Burlington, MA: Pride Publications, Inc.

Bradford, William. *History of Plymouth Plantation, 1606-1646.* William T. Davis (ed.). NY: Charles Scribner's Sons.

Bradford, William. *Of Plymouth Plantation, 1620-1647.* Samuel E. Morison (ed.). NY: Knopf. Reprinted, 1962. NY: Capricorn Books.

Bragdon, Kathleen J. (1996). *Native People of Southern New England, 1500-1650.* Norman, OK: University of Oklahoma Press.

Burkhard, Bilger (1991). "Keeping our Words." *The Sciences,* Sept./Oct.

Champlain, Samuel de. (1613). *Les Voyages du Sieur de Champlain.* Reprinted 1822. *The Works of Champlain.* H.P. Biggar (ed.). Toronto: The Cahmplain Society.

Chief Spotted Eagle (no date). "Language Lessons." Providence, RI: The Algonquin Indian School, Rhode Island Indian Council.

Church, Benjamin (1716). *Entertaining Passages Relating To King Philip's War, Which Began In The Month Of June, 1675; As Also Of Expeditions, More Lately Made Against The Common Enemy, And Indians In The Eastern Part Of New England.* Thomas Church (comp.). Boston: B. Green.

Coombs, Linda. (1992). *Powwow.* Cleveland, OH: Modern Curriculum Press, Inc.

Copi, Irving M. (1978). *Introductory Logic* (5th Ed.) NY: Macmillan Publishing Co., Inc.

Cotton, Josiah (1830). "Vocabulary of the Massachusetts (Natick) Indian Language." Cambridge, MA: *Massachusetts Historical Society Collection, Serial 3, Vol. II.*

Day, Gordon (1995). *Western Abenaki Dictionary. Vol. 2: English-Abenaki.* Quebec: Canadian Museum of Civilization.

Denys, Nicholas (1672). *The Description & Natural History of the Coasts of North America.* Reprinted 1908, William F. Ganong (editor & translator). Toronto: The Champlain Society.

Drake, Samuel (1853). *The Book of Indians of North America.* Boston: Josiah Drake.

Earle, John M. (1821). *Report to the Governor and Council Concerning the Indians of the Commonwealth.* Boston, MA: William White.

Eliot, John (1663). *The Holy Bible: Containing the Old Testament and New Translated into the Indian Language by John Eliot.* Cambridge, MA: Samuel Green and Marmaduke Johnson. (second edition, 1685.)

Eliot, John (1666). *The Indian Grammar Begun; or, an Essay to Bring The Indian Language into Rules for the Help of Such as Desire to Learn the Same for the Furtherance of the Gospel Among Them.* Cambridge, MA.

Eliot, John & Thomas Mayhew (1653). "Tears of repentance: or, A further Narrative of the Progress of the Gospel Amongst the Indians in New-England". London: Peter Cole. Reprinted in *Collections of the Massachusetts Historical Society,* 3rd. ser. vol. 4, 1834, pp. 197-287.

Erhardt, John G. (1992a). *The History of Rehoboth, Seekonk, East Providence, Pawtucket and Barrington.* Vol. 1: *Seacunke,* 1500s to 1645. Seekonk, MA: J.G. Erhardt.

Erhardt, John G. (1992b). *The History of Rehoboth, Seekonk, East Providence, Pawtucket and Barrington.* Vol. 2: *Rehoboth, Plymouth Colony,* 1645-1692. Seekonk, MA: J.G. Erhardt.

Erhardt, John G. (1992c). *The History of Rehoboth, Seekonk, East Providence, Pawtucket and Barrington.* Vol. 3: *A History of Rehoboth, Seekonk, Massachusetts, Pawtucket, and East Providence,* 1692-1812. Seekonk, MA: J.G. Erhardt.

Goddard, Ives (1978). "Eastern Algonquian languages." In Bruce Trigger (ed.), *Handbook of North American Indians, vol.* 15 *(Northeast),* pages 70-77.

Goddard, Ives (1981). "Massachusett Phonology: A Preliminary Look." In *Papers of the Twelfth Algonquian Conference,* ed. William Cowan, 57-105. Ottawa: Carlton University.

Goddard, Ives (Volume Editor, 1996). *Handbook of North American Indians, vol.* 17 *(Languages).* Washington, DC: Smithsonian Institution.

Goddard, Ives and Kathleen J. Bragdon (1988). *Native Writings in Massachusett (Parts* 1 & 2). Philadelphia: The American Philosophical Society.

Gookin, Daniel (1674, 1792). *Historical Collections Of The Indians Of New England: Of Their Several Nations, Numbers, Customs, Manners, Religion, And Government, Before The English Planted There.* New York: Reprinted Edition (1972), Arno Press.

Haffenreffer, Jr., R. F. (1927). "Indian History of Mount Hope and Vicinity". *Proceedings of Fall River Historical Society.*

Handlin, Oscar, and others (eds.) (1955). *Harvard Guide To American History.* Cambridge, MA: Belknap Press, Harvard University.

Haupmann, Lawrence H. & James D. Wherry. (1990). *The Pequots of Southern New England: The Fall and Rise of an American Indian Nation.* Univ. of Oklahoma Press.

Hertzberg, Hazel. (1971). *The Search for an American Indian Identity: Modern Pan Indian Movements.* NY: Syracuse Univ. Press.

Higginson, Francis (1630). *New-England Plantation* or *a short and true DESCRIPTION of the Commodities and Discommodities of that Country.* London.

Huden, John C. (1962). *Indian Place Names of New England.* NY: Heye Foundation.

Jennings, Francis (1975). *The Invasion of America: Indians, Colonialism and the Cant of Conquest*. Chapel Hill, NC: Univ. of North Carolina Press.

Jennings, Paula Dove. (1992). *Strawberry Thanksgiving*. Cleveland, OH: Modern Curriculum Press, Inc.

Josselyn, John (1674, 1675). *Two Voyages to New-England, 1638 & 1663*. Reprinted 1833 in *Collections of Massachusetts Historical Society*.

Kaiser, Mrs. Karl W. (no date). *Musical Expressions of Early Rhode Island Indians, by Mrs. Karl W. Kaiser as Told by Princess Red Wing*. Rhode Island Federation of Music.

Kretch, Shepard. K. (ed.) (1994). *Passionate Hobby: Rudolph Frederick Haffenreffer and the King Philip Museum*. Studies in Anthropology and Material Culture, Vol. VI. Bristol, RI: Haffenreffer Museum of Anthropology, Brown University.

Lenz, Peter A. (1994). *Volume I, Voyages to Norumbega, c 997 - 1626*. Norway, ME: Maine Performing Arts and Humanities, Inc.

Lenz, Peter A. (1995a). *Skicinuwok Wanbanaghi or People of the Aurora, 1621-1625, vol. 2, Part 1*. Norway, ME: Maine Performing Arts and Humanities, Inc.

Lenz, Peter A. (1995b). *Skicinuwok Wanbanaghi or People of the Aurora, 1621-1625, vol. 2, Part 2*. Norway, ME: Maine Performing Arts and Humanities, Inc.

Lenz, Peter A. (1995c). *Skicinuwok Wanbanaghi: People of the Aurora, 1621-1625, [vol. 2,] Part 3*. Norway, ME: Maine Performing Arts and Humanities, Inc.

Masthay, C. (1987). "New England Place Names". In R.G. Carlson (ed.). *Rooted Like the Ashes: New England Indians and the Land*. (Revised Edition). Naugatuck, CT: Eagle Wing Press, Inc.

Moondancer [Frank O'Brien]. (1990). *Food and Fire: A Collection of Poetry, Analects & Neologisms*. (unpub.).

Moondancer (1996). *Wampumpeag*. Newport, RI: Aquidneck Indian Council.

Moondancer (1996). *Neologisms: A Compilation of Words Suggested for Incorporation into the English Language*. Newport, RI: Aquidneck Indian Council.

Moondancer & Strong Woman (1996). *Understanding Algonquian Indian Words (New England)*. rev. ed. 2001. Newport, Rhode Island: Aquidneck Indian Council.

Moondancer & Strong Woman (1997a). *Contributions of the Wampanoag and New England Indians to America*. Newport, RI: Aquidneck Indian Council.

Moondancer & Strong Woman (1997b). *Understanding Indian Place Names in Rhode Island, Massachusetts and Connecticut*. Newport, RI: Aquidneck Indian Council. (unpub.)

Moondancer & Strong Woman (1999). *Handbook of Indian Place Names in Southeastern New England*. Newport, RI: Aquidneck Indian Council. (unpub.)

Moondancer & Strong Woman (2000). *Indian Grammar Dictionary for N-Dialect: A Study of A Key into the Language of America by Roger Williams, 1643*. Newport, Rhode Island: Aquidneck Indian Council.

Moondancer & Strong Woman (2001). *Introduction to the Narragansett Language: A Study of A Key into the Language of America by Roger Williams, 1643*. Newport, Rhode Island: Aquidneck Indian Council.

Morton, Thomas (1632). *New English Canaan or New Canaan. Containing an Abstract of New England, Composed In Three Books. The First Book setting forth the originall of the Natives, their Manners and Customes, together with their tractable Nature and Love towards the English. The Second Book setting forth the naturall Indowments of the Country, and what staple Commodiities it yealdeth. The third Book setting forth, what people are planted there*. Amsterdam: Jacob Frederick Stam.

Mourt, G. (1622). [*Mourt's Relation*]. *A Relation, or Journal of the Beginning and proceedings of the English Plantation settled at Plymouth; by certian English Adventurers, both Merchants and others*. London.

Narragansett Dawn, Narragansett Tribal Nation, 1935-1936, Oakland, RI.

Nichols, Benjamin R. (1882). "Index to Cotton's Ms. Vocabulary of the Massachusetts (Indian) Language." Boston, MA: Manuscript of the Massachusetts Historical Society.

Noble, Mildred (1997). *Sweetgrass: Lives of Contemporary Native Women of the Northeast*. Greenfield Center, N.Y: Mildred Noble.

O'Brien, Frank Waabu (2003). *American Indian Place Names In Rhode Island: Past & Present*. Newport, Rhode Island.
[http://www.rootsweb.com/~rigenweb/IndianPlaceNames.html]

O'Brien, Frank Waabu (2004). *Bibliography for Studies of American Indians in and Around Rhode Island, 16th -21st Centuries:* © 2004.
http://www.rootsweb.com/~rigenweb/IndianBibliography.html.

O'Brien, Frank Waabu (2005). *New England Algonquian Language Revival: A Series of Articles by Dr. Frank Waabu, Aquidneck Indian Council:* © 2005; http://www.geocities.com/bigorrin.htm, Sept., 2005.

Peirce, Ebenezer W. (1878). *Indian History, Biography & Genealogy: Pertaining to the Good Sachem Massasoit of the Wampanoag Tribe and his Descendants.* North Abinbgton, MA: Zerviah Gould Mitchel.

Peters, Russell M. *(1987). The Wampanoag of Mashpee: An Indian Perspective.* Spiritual and Healing Council.

Peters, Russell M. (1992). *Clambake, A Wampanoag Tradition.* NY: Lehrer Publications.

Pilling, James C. (1891). *Bibliography of the Algonquian Language.* Bureau of American Ethnology, Bulletin 13, Washington, DC.

Princess Red Wing (1986). *What Cheer Netop. History, Culture & Legends of American Indians of the Northeast* (audio-cassette); [copyright Mary Benjamin South Casco, Maine].

Purtill, Richard L. (1971). *Logic for Philosophers.* NY: Harper & Row, Publishers, Inc.

Rasieres, Isaack de. (1628?). *Issack de Rasieres to Samuel Blomaert.* Reprinted, 1963, Sydney V. James (ed.). *Three Visitors to Early Plymouth.* Plymouth, MA: Plimouth Plantation.

Records of the Colony of Rhode Island and Providence Plantations, in New England, Vol I, 1636-1663. Printed in 1856, Providence, RI: A. Crawford Greene and Brother, State Printers.

Records of the Colony of Rhode Island and Providence Plantations, in New England, Vol II, 1664-1677. Printed in 1857, Providence, RI: A. Crawford Greene and Brother, State Printers.

Records of the Colony of Rhode Island and Providence Plantations, in New England, Vol III, 1678-1706. Printed in 1858, Providence, RI: A. Crawford Greene and Brother, State Printers.

Records of the Colony of Rhode Island and Providence Plantations, in New England, Vol IV, 1707-1740. Printed in 1859, Providence, RI: Knowles, Anthony & Co., State Printers.

Records of the Colony of Rhode Island and Providence Plantations, in New England, Vol V, 1741-1756. Printed in 1860, Providence, RI: Knowles, Anthony & Co., State Printers.

Records of the Colony of Rhode Island and Providence Plantations, in New England, Vol VI, 1757-1769. Printed in 1861, Providence, RI: Knowles, Anthony & Co., State Printers.

Rider, S. S. (1904). *The Lands of Rhode Island and Massachusetts as They were known to Counounicus and Miantunnomu When Roger Wiliams Came in 1636.* Providence, RI: S. S. Rider.

Salisbury, Neal. (1974). "Red Puritans: The 'Praying Indians' of Massachusetts Bay and John Eliot." *William & Mary Quarterly,* 3rd. ser., vol. 31, no. 1, pp. 27-54.

Seaver, James E. (1824), *A Narrative of the Life of Mrs. Mary Jemison.* Repinted (1981). Canandaigua: J. D. Demis & Co.

Simmons, William S. (1986). *Spirit of the New England Tribes: Indian History and Folklore, 1620-1984. Hanover, NH: University Press of New England.*

Slotkin, Richard & James. K. Folsom (eds.). (1978). *So Dreadfull a Judgment: Puritan Responses to King Philip's War, 1675-1676.* Middeltown, CT: Wesleyan Press.

Speck, Frank G. (1928). *Territories & Boundaries of the Wampanoag, Massachusett and Nausett Indians, Monograph No. 44.* NY: Heye Foundation.

Strong Woman (1999). *Succotash.* Newport, RI: Aquidneck Indian Council, Inc.

Strong Woman & Moondancer (1998a). "Bringing Back Our Lost Language". *American Indian Culture and Research Journal,* vol. 22, no. 3.

Strong Woman & Moondancer. (1998b)."Our Indian Languages Carved in Stone", *Narragansett Indian News,* vol. 3, no. 4, Apr. 23.

Strong Woman & Moondancer (1998c). *Gatherings: The En'owkin Journal of First North American Peoples,* Vol. IX, Fall.

Strong Woman & Moondancer. (1998d). *A Massachusett Langauge Book, vol.* 1 (First Edition).Newport, RI: Aquidneck Indian Council, Inc.

Travers, Milton A. (1976), *One of the Keys, 1676-1776-1996. The Wampanaog Indians Contribution. A List of Words and Definitions from the Language of the Historical Indians of Southeastern Massachusetts; Cape Cod, Martha's Vineyard, Nantucket and Rhode Island.* The Dartmouth, Massachusetts Bicentennial Commission.

Trigger, Bruce G. (Volume Editor, 1978). *Handbook of North American Indians,* vol. 15 (*Northeast*). Washington, DC: Smithsonian Institution.

Trumbull, James H. (1881, 1974). *Indian Names of Places, etc. in and on the Borders of Connecticut with Interpretation of Some of Them.* Hartford, CT: Lockwood & Brainerd.

Trumbull, James H. (1903). *Natick Dictionary*. Washington, DC: Bureau of American Ethnology.

Verrazano, Giovanni da. *Voyages*. Pages 1-24, in *Sailor's Narratives along the New England Coast 1524-1624*. George Parker Winship (ed.). NY: B. Franklin.

Wilbur, Keith C. (1996). *The New England Indians*. Saybrook, CT: Globe Pequot Press.

Williams, Roger (1643). *A Key into the Language of America:, or, an Help to the Language of the Natives in that Part of America called New-England. Together, with Briefe Observations of the Customes, Manners and Worships, etc. of the Aforesaid Natives, in Peace and Warre, in Life and Death. On all which are added Spirituall Observations, General and Particular by the Author of chiefe and Special use (upon all occasions) to all the English Inhabiting those parts; yet pleasant and profitable to the view of all men*. London: Gregory Dexter.

Winslow, Edward (1624). *Good News from New England* (cited in Lenz, 1995).

Winslow, Edward (Dec., 1621). *A Letter Sent From New England To A Friend In These Parts, Setting Forth A Brief And True Declaration Of The Worth Of That Plantation; As Also Certain Useful Directions For Such As Intend A Voyage Into Those Parts*. (cited in Lenz, 1995a).

Winthrop, John (1630-1649). *Journal: "History of New England."* James Kendall Hosmer (ed.), *Original Narratives in Early American History*, 2 vols. NY: Charles Scribner's Sons.

Wood, William (1634). *New England Prospect. A True, lively, and experimentall description of that part of America, commonly called New England: discovering the state of that countrie, both as it stands to our new-come English Planters; and to the old native inhabitants. Laying down that which may both enrich the knowledge of the mind-travelling Reader, or benefit the future Voyager*. London: Tho. Cotes.

pakodjteau-un
[it is ended]

Wunnohteaonk

MAY PEACE BE IN YOUR HEARTS

About the Authors

Frank Waabu O'Brien (Moondancer) earned his Ph.D. at Columbia. He has authored several books and internet websites on southern New England Indians. Moondancer is former President of the Aquidneck Indian Council, and a member of the Abenaki Tribe and Rhode Island Indian Council.

Julianne Jennings (Strong Woman) is a Nottoway artist and educator. She co-produced the Emmy Award winning PBS documentary *Mystic Voices: The Story of the Pequot War*, and is the author of several books on southern New England Indians. Strong Woman is a graduate student in anthropology at Rhode Island College.

www.ingramcontent.com/pod-product-compliance
Ingram Content Group UK Ltd.
Pitfield, Milton Keynes, MK11 3LW, UK
UKHW041450180426
11946UKWH00013B/143/J